THE
BEST BOOK
On:
Self-Publishing With
create space

by

Byron Mettler

Pleasant words are as an honeycomb, sweet to the soul, and health to the bones.

Proverbs 16:24

Contact Byron at:
booksbybyron@gmail.com
www.booksbybyron.com

ISBN 978-0-9826-8582-2

a UNIKGIFTS publication

Byron's other books:
Speed Kills! - 2008 winner of the Nancy Bayless Award
Out of Darkness
Sixteen Stories by John Howard Ladd:
                          Complied by Byron Mettler
Chandler
Things my Mother Taught Me
I Feel Like Writing Poetry
Oakcreek Adventure
52 Great Bible Object Lessons

THE
BEST BOOK

On:

Self-Publishing
With

createspace

Buy This Book and Get Published!, 5-Stars

October 4, 2011 By -Williams Savage Books

You know you have a book inside you. You know you want to share it with the world. The easiest and most cost-effective way to self-publish right now is by using CreateSpace.com. And to learn all of CreateSpace's tips and tricks you need this book, "Self-Publishing With CreateSpace" by Byron Mettler.

> *If there's a book you really want to read, but it hasn't been written yet, then you must write it.* ~Toni Morrison

Using CreateSpace, you can publish your first book in 30 days for no cost except standard shipping. I know, because that's how I did it.

I don't work for CreateSpace. They pay me nothing except the royalties I earn by selling books.

Feel free to use any vanity publishing company you want and start by forking over hundreds of dollars.

Or, you can do some of the hard work and save yourself tons of money.

And thank *yourself* for buying this book.

✶ ✶ ✶ ✶ ✶

Contents

> *I love being a writer. What I can't stand is the paperwork.*
> *~Peter De Vries*

1

Why Use CreateSpace

Cheap-

Zero. Zilch. Nada. Nothing. You can't beat cheap. You pay no upfront costs.

I thought about naming this book, *Publish Your Book In 30 Days for Free* but figured no one would believe me.

Log on to the CreateSpace at www.createspace.com and you will see a "Publish Your Words Your Way" title.

Click the icon, "Start A Title For Free."

Type in your Project Name. (This can be changed before you submit your project for review.

Select, "Paperback."

Click on the, "Guided" process.

Once there you enter your author name. Type in the book description and follow the prompts to enter information about your book

So far, you haven't spent a dime. And you never have to. When you're ready to purchase your first copy, all you pay is the printing cost, which could be as little as $2.15 for a 108-page book, plus tax, and shipping. Shipping is based on standard USPS shipping rates and does not include a markup cost. See Chapter 6 Uploading for more information on submitting your book information.

Easy-

Easy is a relative statement, especially when it comes to computer software, design, editing and layout. CreateSpace is easy in that their website is easy to navigate and it's easy to upload your book and cover. If you make a mistake with your file format, CreateSpace will send you a note stating what went wrong.

They won't fix your mistakes. They won't check spelling or grammar, or tell you if you have a great cover or a dud. The basic CreateSpace publishing option is a "What You See Is What You Get" type of program.

That's good for you because you have total control over your finished product. Your finished book will only be as good as you. Most of us think we are pretty good fellows, so there's no excuse for a lousy end product. How many times have you read a book and said to yourself, "I can write better than that dope." Now, here's your chance.

Available-

Through my years as a writer, I went through the usual process of typing my manuscript (on one of those old ancient black manual typewriters). Going to the library to look up publishers. Mailing out scores of manuscripts to companies in New York City, because we were told that's where all the good publishers live. And waiting for weeks and months, only to get a rejection form saying, "thanks but we can't use this right now." Occasionally, an editor would leave a handwritten note with a word of encouragement. Thanks whoever you are. I didn't give up.

Today you can contact CreateSpace any time, any day and they will actually respond! Email is the best thing since language was invented

If you want to do more research, you can log on to their website and get tons of free information on how to layout your cover, set up the interior and market your book. They also have a useful "Community" link where serious writers are discussing their progress and successes.

CreateSpace has recently added several Pay For Service options. Feel free to use the services if you need help with layout or editing but you are not required to use any of these services to publish with CreateSpace.

The Next Big Thing-

Bowker Statistics 2009: Non-traditional Means Now The Majority Path For Authors
by Editor on Wednesday, April 14, 2010

The latest 2009 statistical report released by R.R. Bowker today is a real eye-opener. The total amount of titles produced last year was 1,052,803, and significantly, 764,448 of that overall figure came from what Bowker describe as non-traditional channels – a mix of micro-publishers, self-publishers and reprints of public domain titles.

In simple terms, 2010 will see non-traditional produced titles outstrip traditional titles by three to one— something that would have been considered mind-blowing three or four years ago.

"Publishers Weekly announced on-demand published title output up a whopping 132% in 2008 over the previous year whereas traditionally published books down over 3%. The total number of self-published, on-demand books overtook the traditional side for the first year ever last year, demonstrating further the inevitable climate change in the publishing industry."
selfpublishingadvice.wordpress.com/2009/07/31/

"U.S. book production rose and fell in 2008, according to preliminary statistics released this morning by Bowker. The number of new and revised titles produced by traditional production methods fell 3% in 2008, to 275,232, but the number of on-demand and short run titles soared 132%, to 285,394. The on-demand and short run segment is the method typically used by self-publishers as well as online publishers. With the decline in the number of traditional books released last year and the jump in on-demand, the number of on-demand titles topped those of traditional books for the first time. Taken together, total output rose 38%, to 560,626 titles."
By Jim Milliot -- Publishers Weekly, 5/19/2009 7:21:00 AM

New Bowker Statistics Point to Publishing Opportunities

by Donald L. Hughes on 05/22/2011

Self-publishers monitored by Bowker are growing at a rate of over 10 percent per year. CreateSpace led the field, with about 34,000 new titles in 2010. Lulu was in second place with 11,000, followed by Xlibris at 10,700 and AuthorHouse with 8,500 (about 64,000 titles as a group).

In 2009, the top five self-publishers, which also included PublishAmerica, accounted for 57,500 new titles. Remember that self-publishers do not use ISBNs for all of their books, so the ISBN-less books are not included in the totals.

Self-Publishing IS the next big thing in book publishing. On-demand publishing is increasing every year.

I believe there will always be a place in the publishing industry for traditional publishers and I hope bookstores like Barnes and Noble always stay in business. I can waste hours; lost in a bookstore sipping a mocha while perusing books I'd love to buy. Keep the presses rolling Random House!

It Works-

I published my first book in 2007 with Publish America. They did okay with the layout but their business plan lacks integrity.

My purpose is not to dump on other publishing houses, but to show you an affordable way to get published. CreateSpace has set up a program that works. Now, you can get your lifelong writing effort easily published at a reasonable cost. The success of your endeavor is up to you.

The Choice is Yours -

Jeff and Marie Edwards published a compilation of student's stories titled, *The Boy: A Fifth Grade Anthology by Jeff Edwards and Fifth Grade Writers Workshop* and published it with CreateSpace using the standard no cost plan. The book lists for $6.99 and copies were sold to school kids, parents, teachers and writers like me.

The purpose of *The Boy* was not to make a literary statement or a pile of money but to encourage future writers. It was a true labor of devotion to the kids. One day we may see a best seller from one of the fifth grade authors.

Barbara McBride, a 73 year-old author, never thought it possible to publish her inspirational poems until she learned of CreateSpace in 2010. Barbara published a book of twenty three poems and within a few months sold over 300 copies.

Self-Publishing with CreateSpace

> *I'm not a very good writer,*
> *but I'm an excellent rewriter.*
> *~James Michener*

2

Have you got What it Takes!

Guts. Determination. Stick-to-it-tiveness. Pride. Ego. Drive. Spiritual calling.

Whatever it is that makes you a writer must be strong enough to carry you through to the final edit. Along the way, you will face opposition, ridicule, financial trials, personal struggles and computer crashes that would deter Jules Verne if he were alive today.

Being a writer is tough no matter what stage you're in. All of us want to be famous and have a list of best sellers out there. If you were famous, you would have an agent setting up meetings for you with publishers and editors; you'd have a publicist scheduling talk shows and radio interviews for you; as well as editors asking you to get a corrected copy back by tomorrow's deadline.

On top of all that, your readers are expecting you to consistently produce good copy, and you have to do that over and over again every year to stay on top. I'm not even near the top, and I'm already tired.

Successful writers must have stick-to-it-tiveness.

Why Write?

My answer is, "I can't help myself." Inside my brain, I have stories and book outlines ready to go and I just need enough time in front of the keyboard to get them out in readable form. (Thank you Microsoft for spell check.)

I also have a desire to leave a legacy and some family history for those who live on after me. I expect that one hundred years from now, no one will ever know I existed. Perhaps, if there is a book or two with my name on it, a future archeologist will dig it up in a thousand years and I'll be revered as a great philosopher of ancient times. You never know.

You have to understand why you write. The journey from keyboard to print is a minefield of problems and disasters. I venture to say that there is not an honest writer out there who will say it's easy.

Why Do You Write?

Now, there's a question to ask yourself.

Be honest. Why do you want to write a novel, short story, memoir, self-help book, poetry collection, advice book, how-to guide, devotional, theological work, sermon collection, visual aid book, or whatever else interests you.

Your reason for writing is the motivation that will help you succeed.

"Love. In short, book-writing is a worse-than-ever means to a livelihood, and mass-market renown is disappearing as a concept, fractioning into a million niches.

Ultimately the only good reason to write books remains what it probably always was: The compulsion to try to entertain, persuade or make meaning is irresistible, and the process absorbs you like nothing else. If it doesn't, there's no reason to bother."

Why Write Books? Elisabeth Eaves,
Notes on BookExpo America.

When I speak with aspiring authors at a book signing or writers seminar, I always try to get the point home that "Your First Book Will Not Be Your Only Book And May Not Be Your Best Book."

I start a book, because I want to get it finished. Along the way, I struggle, faint, give up and start again. It is not unusual for me to lay a manuscript down for weeks, months or even years until I find the right combination of character and plot.

Time- Our Nemesis

I have heard it said that if you take a million monkeys and place them in a large room with a million typewriters for a million years, one of them will eventually write a novel.

I'm just one monkey with one typewriter so I gotta get clicking.

There are those of you who have a gift of sitting down at the keyboard and casually typing out fifty words a minute with 99% accuracy and spend the rest of the day watching Oprah while snacking on Pringles. The rest of us fight the keyboard at every word at it slick out spellig and grammer eerrosa thatw never intended to put there. (That's exactly the way I typed it).

If you are one of those who still have full time employment, you are at a greater disadvantage. Work takes time, mental energy and physical resources. It's nearly impossible to put out a creative, imaginative work when you are exhausted from crunching numbers or dealing with personnel issues all day.

So, you have to find the time when you can write.

No Rules!

Years ago, when I started reading books on writing and publishing, I read in Writers Digest that to be a good writer I had to write at least one hour every day. I agree that most good writers, who have the time, will probably spend an hour or so putting out something.

When I'm in the zone, I can spend tireless hours filling my screen with reasonably good prose.

But I have had months and years of nothing, which is worse because I still have all those thoughts and outlines taking up disk space in my head.

When you have the time, get down to writing. As a self-published author, you won't have an agent or editor pressuring you with demanding deadlines. That's good because it frees up your mind for creating good ideas but bad because it's easy to become lackadaisical.

Do not put statements in the negative form.

And don't start sentences with a conjunction.

If you reread your work, you will find on rereading that a great deal of repetition can be avoided by rereading and editing.

Never use a long word when a diminutive one will do.

Unqualified superlatives are the worst of all.

De-accession euphemisms.

If any word is improper at the end of a sentence, a linking verb is.

Avoid trendy locutions that sound flaky.

Last, but not least, avoid cliches like the plague.
~William Safire, "Great Rules of Writing"

Don't tell me the moon is shining; show me the glint of light on broken glass. ~Anton Chekhov

3

How Much Will You Earn – Big Bucks (maybe)

Examples on cost

CreateSpace offers a low fixed price which will cost you nothing, zip, zero, nada for startup fees. This is a great option if you want to get a book published and you don't have a pile of cash to invest.

At CreateSpace, a 108-page book will cost you $2.15. This applies to all trim sizes, black and white interior, full color cover, paperback, perfect-bound.

A 150-page book will cost you $2.65.
A 175-page book will cost you $2.96.
A 200-page book will cost you $3.26.
A 250-page book will cost you $3.85.
A 300-page book will cost you $4.45.

Member Order Calculator

		Per Book	Order Subtotal
Interior Type	Black and Whi ▼		
Trim Size	5" x 8" ▼		
Number of Pages	175	**$2.96**	**$88.80**
Quantity	30	each	30 copies
Calculate			

* Figures generated by this tool are for estimation purposes only. Your actual order costs will be calculated when you set up your book. This does not include shipping and handling, which can be calculated below.

Order Shipping Calculator

		Shipping Options		
Quantity	30	$18.00	**Standard**	5 business days
Country	U.S. - Continen ▼	$39.99	**Expedited**	2 business days
Calculate		$87.99	**Priority**	1 business days

* See the rate tables used to calculate shipping and handling.
* Shipping times do not include the printing of your order.

The cost has remained constant since I started self-publishing in 2009. You can use the Cost calculator at https://www.createspace.com/Products/Book/ and click on "Buying Copies" to calculate the cost of printing and shipping.

Here is the formula. $0.85 fixed cost plus .012 per page

The same cost applies if you buy one copy or if you buy a thousand books. Shipping is extra. I recently purchased 75 books and paid $41 for shipping. Shipping for a single copy will be about $3.60.

Expanded Distribution

CreateSpace charges a one-time fee of $25 for Expanded Distribution, but you only pay if you decide to choose the expanded distribution option. You can select this option at a later time

These additional sales channels make your book available for order to online retailers, bookstores, libraries, academic institutions, and distributors within the United States.

I selected the Expanded Distribution Channel and soon found my books for sale on the Barnes and Noble online site and available for order at major retail outlets.

Electing to use Expanded Distribution will change your royalty amount.

Sales Channel Percentage

A sales channel percentage is deducted from your book's list price depending on which sales channel the book is sold through.

Sales Channel Percentage	
Standard Distribution - CreateSpace eStore	20% of list price
Standard Distribution - Amazon.com	40% of list price
Expanded Distribution	60% of list price

Royalty Calculator*
Use the royalty calculator to figure out how much you'll make every time your book is manufactured.

Print Options

| Interior Type | Black and White | ▾ | Number of Pages | 262 |
| Trim Size | 5" x 8" | ▾ | | |

List Price			Channel	Royalty
			Amazon.com	$2.00
USD $ 9.99		Calculate	eStore	$4.00
			Expanded Distribution	$0.00
☑ Yes, suggest GBP price based on the U.S. price			Amazon Europe	£0.41
GBP £ 6.22		Calculate	For books printed in Great Britain	
☑ Yes, suggest EUR price based on the U.S. price			Amazon Europe	€0.92
EUR € 7.77		Calculate	For books printed in continental Europe	

When you select Expanded Distribution, the minimum price you can set for your 262 page, black and white book is $9.99. The Royalty Calculator shows that when your book is purchased from your Createspace eStore, you receive $4.00. If it is purchased from Amazon you receive $2.00. When a retailer or distributor purchases your book, your royalty is $.00.

In order to make a profit on every sale, you need to set your price for a 262 page book higher than $9.99.

Go to https://www.createspace.com/Products/Book/ and click on "Distribution and Royalties" to use this calculator.

Full Color Books

Full-color books with 24-40 pages	$3.65 per book
Full-color books with 42-500 pages	$0.85 per book
Full-color books with 42-500 pages	$0.07 per page

Member Order Calculator

Interior Type	Full Color ▾	Per Book	Order Subtotal
Trim Size	6" x 9" ▾		
Number of Pages	42	**$3.79**	**$113.70**
Quantity	30	each	30 copies
	Calculate		

* Figures generated by this tool are for estimation purposes only. Your actual order costs will be calculated when you set up your book. This does not include shipping and handling, which can be calculated below.

Order Shipping Calculator

Quantity	30	**Shipping Options**		
Country	U.S. - Continen ▾	$18.00	**Standard**	5 business days
		$39.99	**Expedited**	2 business days
	Calculate	$87.99	**Priority**	1 business days

* See the rate tables used to calculate shipping and handling.
* Shipping times do not include the printing of your order.

A full color, 42-page book will cost you $3.79 per book. Shipping in the continental US for 30 books will cost $18.00, or .60 (cents) per book. The cost for printing and shipping an 8" x 10", 42-page full color book remains the same.

How to make more money

Make sure you own your rights to:
Movies
Audio

Reprints

E-books

Using Create Space, you own ALL the rights.

CreateSpace allows YOU to set your royalty return.

You can receive a royalty of 0% to 100% or more of each book you publish.

> **CreateSpace tip**
> Books
> You set the list price for your book, and depending on what sales channels you choose, CreateSpace and/or Amazon sets the selling price of your title to customers.
> For books sold to customers, your royalty equals the list price you set in your member account minus our share.
> Our share is calculated by taking a percentage of the list price, plus a fixed charge, plus a charge per page.
> The percentage varies depending on the sales channels you choose for your book.

Here's the key

My book, *Chandler* is a 262-page book and each book costs me $3.99. The minimum retail price CreateSpace allows me to set for resale is $6.66 per book. If I decide to sell my book for the *minimum retail price* my royalty will be the amount shown below.

As you can see, I will make no royalty if my book is purchased on the regular Amazon website.

<u>If a customer buys my book through my CreateSpace e-store my profit is:</u>

Selling cost at $6.57.
Less CreateSpace take of 20% ($1.32) less the cost of printing equals a royalty of $1.33.

$6.66	Selling price
-1.34	CreateSpace take
-3.99	Printing cost (The same as my cost)
$1.33	My royalty

Royalty Calculator*

Use the royalty calculator to figure out how much you'll make every time your book is manufactured.

		eStore	Amazon.com	Expanded Distribution
List Price	6.66	**Your Royalty**		
Interior Type	Black and Whi ▾			
Trim Size	5" x 8" ▾	$1.33	$0.00	-$1.33
Number of Pages	262			
Calculate		**Our Share**		
		$5.33 Details	$6.66 Details	$7.99 Details

* Figures generated by this tool are for estimation purposes only. Your actual royalty will be calculated when you set up your book.

When I decide to sign up for the Expanded Distribution option, I will need to raise my price by $1.33 before I make a profit.

<u>When a customer buys through Amazon my profit is:</u>

Selling cost at $6.57.
Less Amazon take of 40% ($2.63).
Less the cost of printing.
My royalty is $00

$6.66	Selling price
-2.67	Amazon take
<u>-3.99</u>	Printing cost
$.00	My royalty

Amazon charges 40% per book while CreateSpace only charges 20% per book. However, the minimum price is set up for the Amazon profit structure so the list price can never fall below the minimum price.

The author can set any price above the minimum. CreateSpace gives me the freedom to set the price for my books. I can change the price at any time and set promotional discounts for bookstores, non-profit organizations, special sales or friends.

Be aware that if you have chosen the Expanded Distribution Plan you minimum book price for a 262 page book must be at least $9.99.

And, I can set varied discounts.

Createspace will automatically set up a free webpage for you to use, for each book you publish. Your royalties are higher when you direct buyers to purchase your books from your personal CreateSpace eStore. You can also provide your buyers with a unique discount, just for them, if they buy from your CreateSpace eStore.

As an example, you can buy my books at a 30% discount by going to my *Chandler* webpage at the CreateSpace store and enter the following codes.

https://www.createspace.com/3394717
Chandler   30% discount enter
4XRSCPGV

For a 30% discount on *Out of Darkness*, follow the enclosed link and enter the code KYMWAJTZ.
https://www.createspace.com/3393420
Out of Darkness   30% discount enter
KYMWAJTZ

For a 30% discount on *Sixteen Stories by John Howard Ladd*, follow the enclosed link and enter the code KYMWAJTZ.

https://www.createspace.com/3392483
Sixteen Stories by John Howard Ladd 30% discount enter
NW3PSEJV

I like to offer a 45% discount for non-profit organizations and bookstores that buy multiple copies. When visiting schools I can offer a 30% discount off the cover.

I can change this to a 20% discount by providing a different code for the purchase *Out of Darkness* at a 20% discount. Go to:

www.createspace.com/3393420
enter code **MKHTJXT4.**

Instead of paying $11.99 you will pay $9.60. My royalty went from $6.70 to $4.30. CreateSpace still makes 20% of the suggested list price plus the cost of printing the book.

Selling at full price through CreateSpace

$11.99	Selling price
-2.40	CreateSpace take
<u>-2.89</u>	Printing cost
$6.70	My royalty

Selling at full price through Amazon

$11.99	Selling price
-4.80	Amazon take
<u>-2.89</u>	Printing cost
$4.20	My royalty

I listed two examples to show you how easy it is to set varied discounts. As you can see, selling through Amazon reduces the royalty amount, but it is still far better than the 5 to 8% royalty offered to authors by most traditional publishers.

Setting your price

It's up to you to set the final sales price. Using CreateSpace you can change the sales price at any time at no additional cost to you.

If you are selling a specialty book, or have a guaranteed clientele, you will have the freedom to set the price as high as the market will allow.

CreateSpace tip

As a member with direct deposit payment option set up with CreateSpace, we want you to have the most current information regarding royalty payment terms.

Your direct deposit minimum payment threshold amount is now $10/£10/ €10 (previously $20) and the new payment terms will be effective for payments made in June 2012, for any royalties earned through May.

In addition, with direct deposit, currency conversion is now available. This means if you have a bank account in the U.S., U.K., Germany, France, Spain, Portugal, Belgium, or the Netherlands you can be paid in either U.S. dollars, British pounds, or Euro.

Other payment changes have been made regarding checks. If you choose not to select direct deposit for your royalty payments and have checks sent to the U.S., U.K., Germany, France, Spain, Portugal, Belgium, or the Netherlands, then a check handling fee of $8/£8/€8 will apply per payment. The payment by check will increase to a minimum payment amount of $100/£100/€100.

How to lose money

1. Write a terrible book.

2. Publish your book before it is complete.

3. Publish before the editing is complete.

4. Pay too much for the cover.

5. Pay too much for editing.

6. Pay too much to self-publish.

7. Hire a publicist who offers a service you are not ready for.

> *It took me fifteen years to discover I had no talent for writing, but I couldn't give it up because by that time I was too famous.* ~Robert Benchley

4

What You See Is What You Get

This chapter covers the nuts and bolts and loose screws of the CreateSpace process.

As the title states **WHATYOUSEEISWHATYOUGET**.

You the Writer

Your book is all the world will know of you. Each line will be judged, criticized and enjoyed by your readers. It's up to you to make it right. Take time to re-read and re-edit every line to create the best product you are capable of.

You the Editor

I'll leave it up to you to hone your work but I will give you a few tips on editing. If you know a good editor, hire them to help you. A skilled read from an outside source is an excellent way to fix flaws you will never find.

If you act as your own editor, expect to invest at least twice as much time with the editing as you did for your first draft. Your skill and experience with grammar and sentence structure will determine the readability of your book.

You the Designer

As a publisher, you are responsible for every part of your book. I read the credits in the forwards of a few books recently and discovered that many nationally published books are the work of numerous experts in book publishing. Some of the job titles listed are: Publisher, Product Manager, Senior Acquisitions Editor,

Development Editor, Production Editor, Copy Editor, Illustrator, Cover Designer, Book Designer, Indexer, Layout and Proofreader.

Get your jumbo size hat rack out because you wear all the hats.

You the Agent

Using traditional publishing, you will finish your manuscript or proposal, print a copy and send it to an agent and wait for a response. But how do you find the right agent?

"Ah, there's the rub," as Shakespeare said. I bought a book recently titled, *Guide to Literary Agents* with "over 250,000 copies sold" stamped on the cover. The book lists hundred of agents broken down by category with eighty how-to pages of instructions on manuscript submission.

Stop right here. You are your agent. You've decided to self-publish so you don't have to spend hundreds of hours on submissions to agents who have no interest in your manuscript. Seven months ago, I sent one of my books to an interested agent and I am still waiting for a response. In that time, I published four books.

You the Marketer

Marketing is the first thing, the middle thing and the last thing you should do as a self-published author.

The general public has the misconception that a publisher signs an author and automatically invests thousands of dollars in marketing by producing slick color ads and scheduling TV appearances. And they do it all for free.

Publishing companies will sometimes do limited marketing for well-known authors but the cost is taken out of their advance as a pre-payment of royalties. It's the author's money they are spending.

To help you to build a great marketing plan for your book, buy *Gorilla Marketing For Authors* and READ it. This book will stimulate you to explore new markets in ways you have never dreamed. Most authors will do everything but marketing. Without marketing, 99% of unknown author will remain unknown.

You first heard about this book from some form of marketing. It may have been a book signing, author interview, web page or by word of mouth. Your marketing plan, or lack of, will impact your degree of success.

You the Bookseller

Selling books is what it's all about. Your sales strategy should include the brass tacks, nitty gritty, bare essentials and nuts and bolts of your plan. Before you write the first line, decide who your book is for. Don't compromise what's in your heart but as you write, visualize your intended audience reclining in an easy chair, near a golden fire, reading your printed words.

Determine where your audience shops and place your books where your readers will see it. Borders Books, Barnes and Nobel and other brick and mortar stores save their prime end caps for the best selling authors.

You might think to yourself, *If only I had my book on an end cap in a major store, I would be a best selling author.* Maybe, maybe not. But without a major name on the cover or a successful movie deal, your book will probably sit there quietly collecting dust.

All the other books lined up side-by-side on the shelves are simply called "wallpaper."

I looked up the sales requirement for Borders Books and discovered they own about 600 bookstores. To be reordered, any book on the shelf must sell at least two copies per year, per store. That's 1,200 books per year. Even if you are shelved in a major bookstore, there is no guarantee you will make a profit. Borders sells books to make money for the corporation, not for authors.

Your Job Titles

If you want to know what it takes to publish a book in the national market, read the forward from one of Max Lucado's books to see how many people worked to publish one book. One of his forwards listed at least twenty people who had a part in the book's success.

Remember, you are all of those people. You are the author, researcher, cover artist, layout expert, editor, grammar checker, page designer, fact checker, publisher, marketer, advertising executive and therapist. You may be fortunate to hire assistance in many of these areas but it will still be your responsibility to make the final executive decisions.

Software Primer

You need the right tools for the right job.

Computer: If your computer is more than six years old, you may need to replace the whole system to keep up with new technology.

You will be pleased to know you don't have to spend $699 to purchase Adobe Photoshop to format your book. If you have access to Photoshop and you are really smart, then go for it. I tried a free version but found a bug with converting Word documents to Photoshop, so I dumped it and use Word to prepare my manuscript.

I use:

✧ MS Word 2007 to write my book and format the pages.

✧ You can use the MS Word 2003 version also

✧ Scan Soft PDF Professional to convert the Word document to a PDF file

✧ Printshop Pro Publisher to create the book cover and save it as a PDF file.

✧ Photo Impact Pro to edit photos used on my covers.

My total cost for software is less than $500. Word 2007 already has a PDF converter, so if you own this version you will save a step.

Book Layout using MS Word 97-2003
(See the end of this chapter for Word 2007 tips)
Page Size

CreateSpace offers standard trim sizes, which include:

  * 5.25" x 8"
  * 5.5" x 8.5"
  * 6" x 9"
  * 7" x 10"
  * 8" x 10"
  * 8.25" x 8.25"
  * 8.25" x 6"

More sizes are available. Before setting up your manuscript for publication, you have to decide what size book you want. For novels, you will use the smaller sizes.

For poetry, picture books and how-to books, you should select a larger size.

Using MS Word for a typical 5.25 x 8 book, you should do the following. Double click "File," Go to Page Setup.

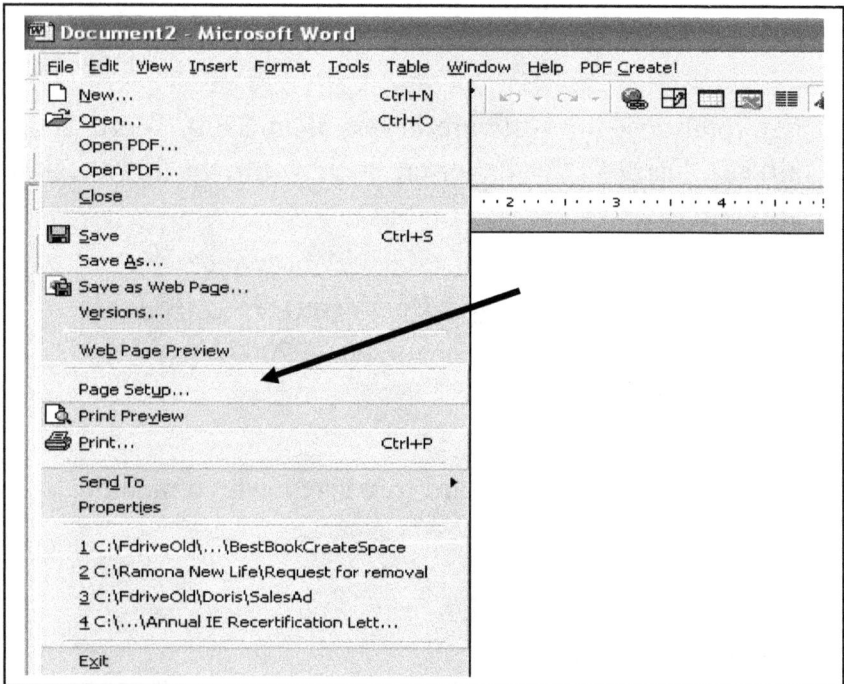

Enter Width 5.25 and Height 8". Click "Portrait".

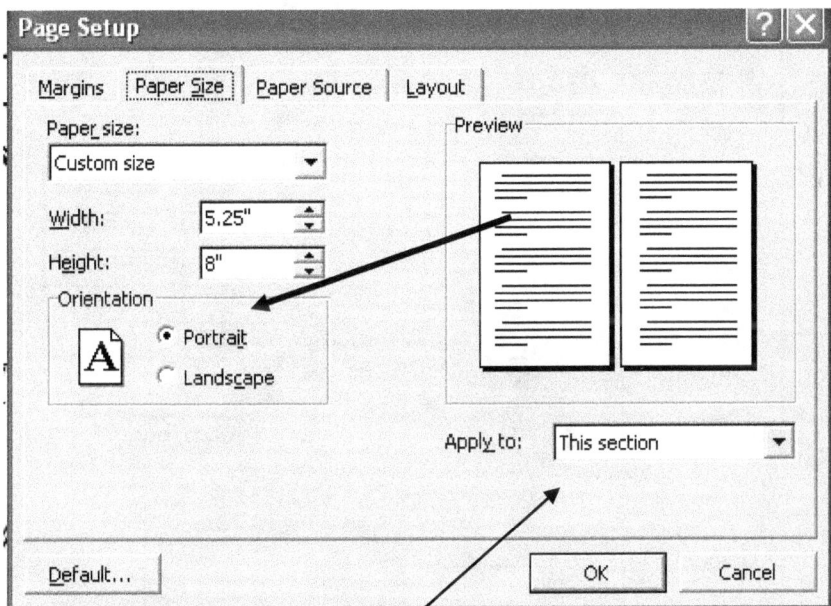

Change "This Section" to "Whole Document".

Set your **Margins**

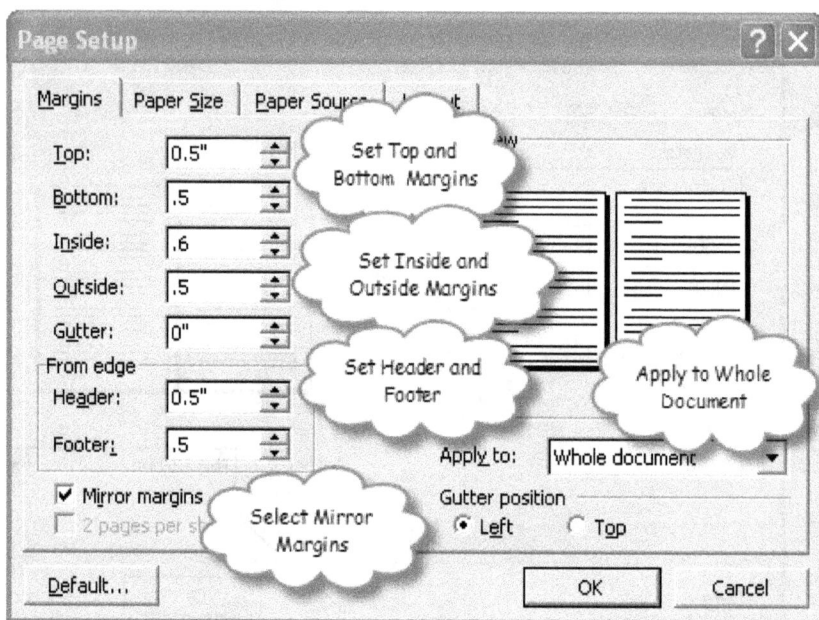

Be sure to set "Mirror Margins" to provide more room on the inside of the page for binding. If you want more white space around your text, increase the margin until you are satisfied with the results. Remember, you are the publisher. You have total control of how your printed book will look.

The book you are reading is printed on 6-inch by 9-inch paper. The top, bottom and inside margins are 1-inch. The outside margin is .75-inch. The header and footer are .5-inch. The gutter is 0.

For the **Font**, I use Times New Roman at 13 pt.

For line spacing, I use "At least" 16 pt. If your manuscript is already finished, click Select All then select Paragraph and set your line spacing and font size. If you have previously formatted some of the chapter titles with a different font, you will have to reformat them.

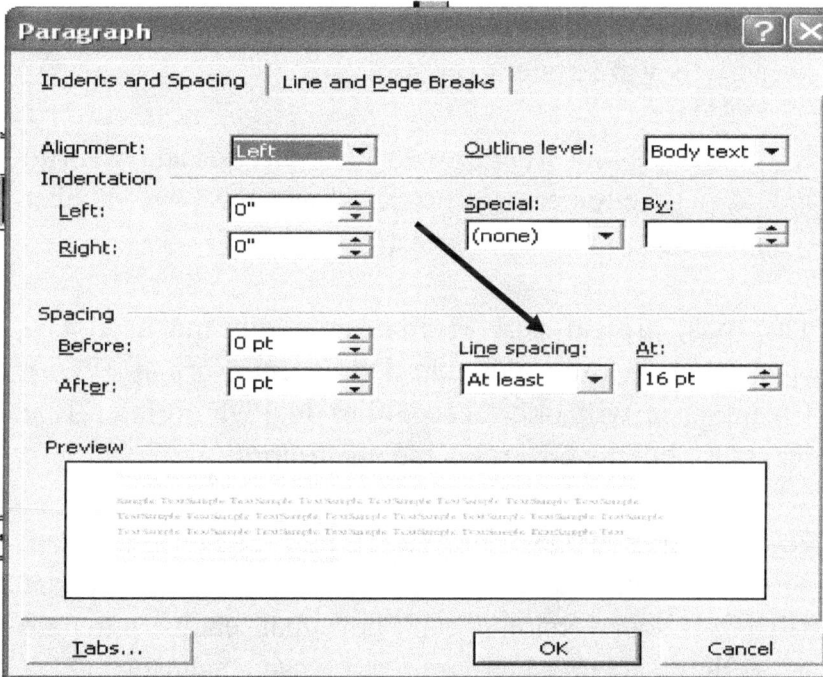

Going back to the "What You See Is What You Get" idea, you will learn that your book will print exactly the way it shows on your computer screen. I like to set my View - Zoom to 90% so I can see two pages side-by-side. Often, I will reduce it to 60% to see four pages at once, so I will know how the pages appear in relation to each other.

It's your job to set the indents, Page Breaks, Numbering, Headers, Footers, Page notes and the unique details you want in your book. I suggest you find a published book you like and copy the style.

You can add almost any element in your book that you can create in your MS Word document.

I often use Text Boxes to insert photos or graphics because they are easier to control.

If you are having trouble with Page Breaks and want to hide a page number or a header, cover the page number with a white text box and select "no line".

The most critical part of finishing your manuscript is converting it to a Portable Document Format (PDF). CreateSpace will only accept files in PDF format. That includes both the cover and the manuscript.

Some version of MS Word have a PDF converter built in, so all you have to do is select "Save As" and choose "PDF". If your version doesn't have that feature, purchase a PDF converter program. I use Scansoft PDF Professional 4. Warning: Do not make Scansoft PDF your default PDF viewer. It will try to take over your system and slow down your computer.

Embed Fonts

Before you convert your file to PDF, you must embed the fonts.

> **CreateSpace tip**
> Font
>
> Embed font information. Do not use Type 3 fonts as they cause problems at the RIP and can cause the file not to print.

In MS Word you select "Tools" "Option" check "Embed True Type Fonts" then "OK".

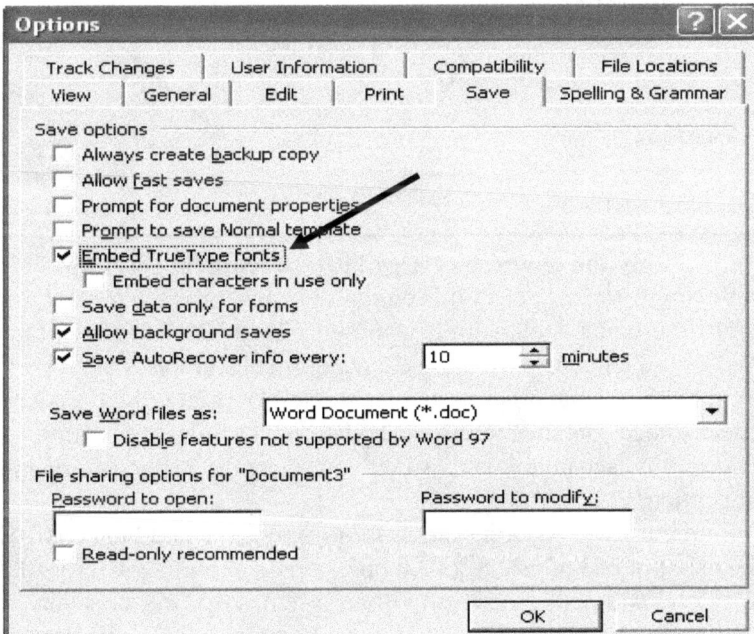

To embed fonts using Word 2007, you need to click the Save As option and select embed fonts from the Tools menu.

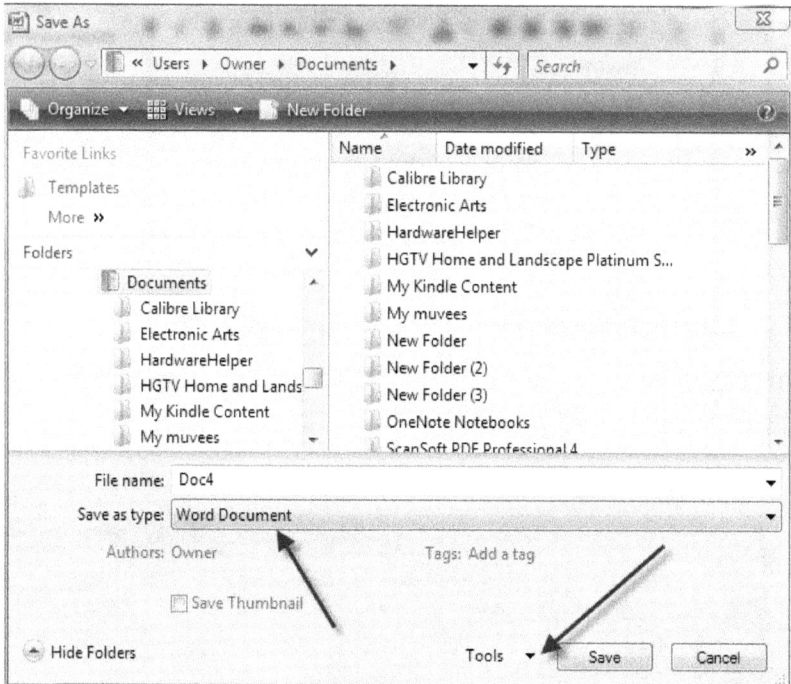

Embed only the characters used in the document (best for reducing file size) Select this option to embed only the fonts that you actually use in a document. If you use 32 or fewer characters of a font, Word embeds only those characters. This option is most useful for documents that other users plan to view or print only, because the unembedded font characters and styles aren't available for editing. This option is available only when you select the Embed fonts in the file option.

Do not embed common system fonts Select to embed fonts only if they are not commonly installed on computers running Microsoft Windows and 2007 Microsoft Office system software. This option is available only when you select the Embed fonts in the file option.

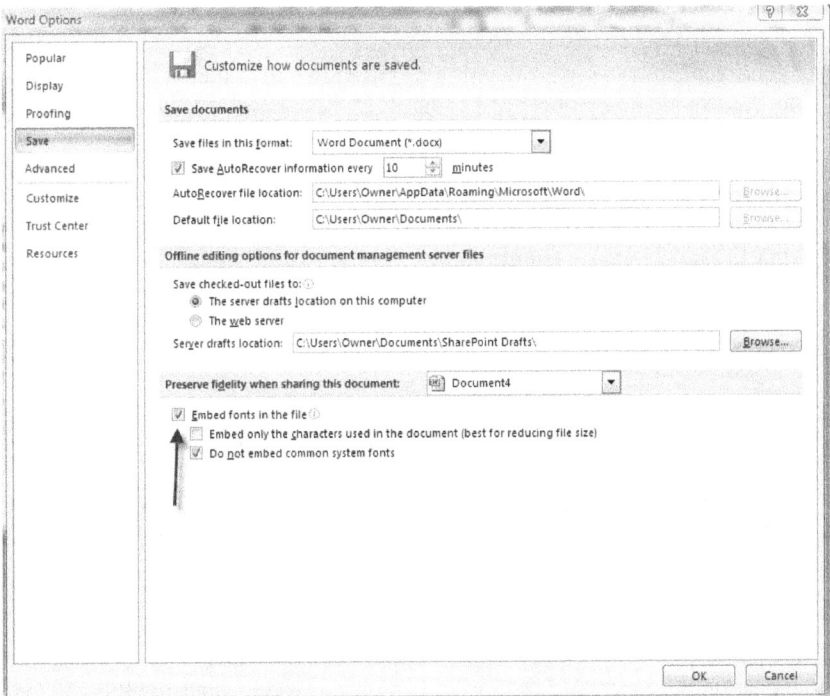

Fonts will be one of those loose screws I mentioned earlier. There are many fonts that do not want to embed in your document. I don't know why, but I discovered that when I sent my book, *I Feel Like Writing Poetry* to CreateSpace for publication. In this book, I used twenty-eight different fonts to add interest to the poems.

I saved it as PDF with embed fonts function checked but some fonts still would not embed properly.

no_reply@createspace.com is a notification only e-mail address that does not receive incoming or reply messages

The files for I Feel Like Writing Poetry have been reviewed and do not meet the submission specifications for the reason(s) listed below. Please make any necessary adjustments to your files and upload them again by logging in to your CreateSpace member account.

Before uploading new files, you may wish to review the Submission Requirements, available at: https://www.createspace.com/Products/Book/

The interior file contains the font Ruachlet is not embedded that we are unable to embed. You will need to embed all fonts in your PDF file.

The spine text is too large for the page count. We recommend reducing the font size and centering the spine text so there is at least 1/16 of room on either side. Otherwise, the spine text may wrap to the front or back cover.

The cover contains live elements that may be trimmed. Please make sure that the text appears .375" away from the outer edges. All elements you wish to appear on the cover, such as text and graphics, need to appear within the live graphics area. Only background that can be cut off should extend through the bleed area.

As you can see, this project had a few design problems. CreateSpace was generous to tell me about them so I could make the corrections. Because I used so many different fonts in this book, it was sent back six times for corrections. I don't know why CreateSpace did not provide a complete list on the first review.

You not only have to embed the fonts using MS Word but also may have to select the embed font option in your PDF converter. Scansoft PDF Professional 4 has an option to select "Embed Fonts".

Always remember to embed your fonts. Tuck them in and put them to sleep in your manuscript so the printer can wake them up when needed.

Word 2007 Tips

MS Word 2007 Menu

Double click "Page Layout" and scroll down to select 'Margins." Scroll down and select "Custom margins."

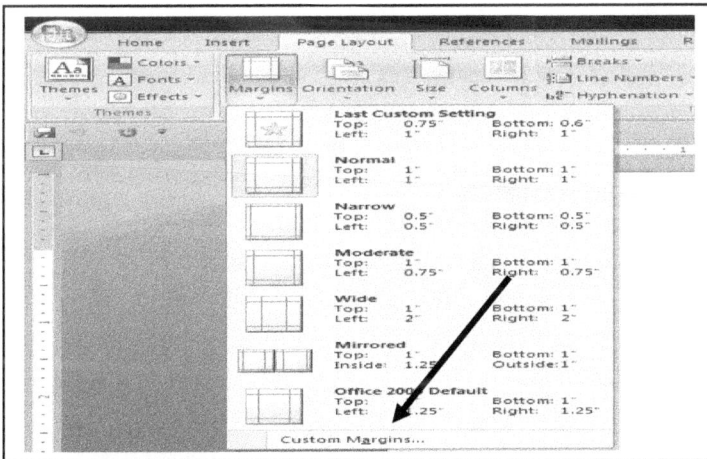

Select your margins.
The inside margin should be larger than the outside.

Select "Mirror Margins" which will always keep the large margin on the spine side.

In most cases, you will select "Whole document."
Keep the header and footer the same size unless you want more white space on the top or bottom of the page.

Page Setup

While in Custom Margins select "Paper." Set the width and height of your page and click "Okay."

On Multiple Pages select "Mirror Margins."

Select "Whole Document."

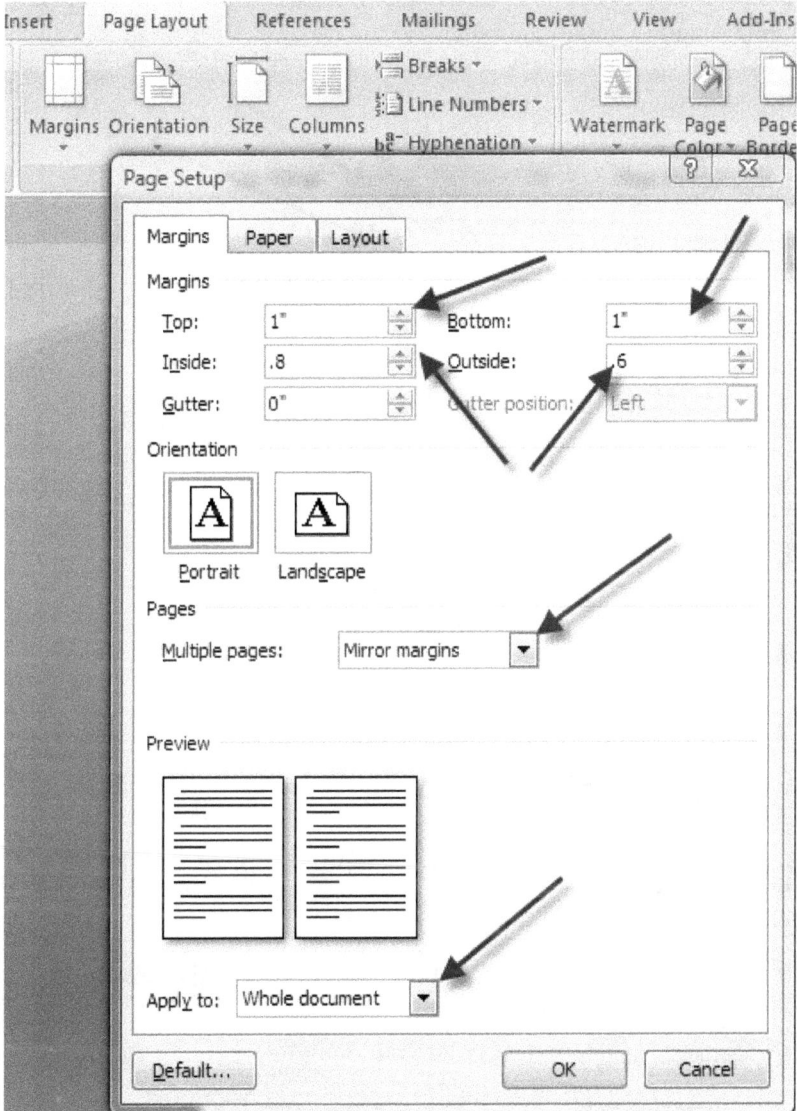

Use this screen to Select Margins, page Orientation and apply to Whole Document.

Many of the command functions in 2007 are accessed through the picture icons rather than the right click button commonly used on the older versions.

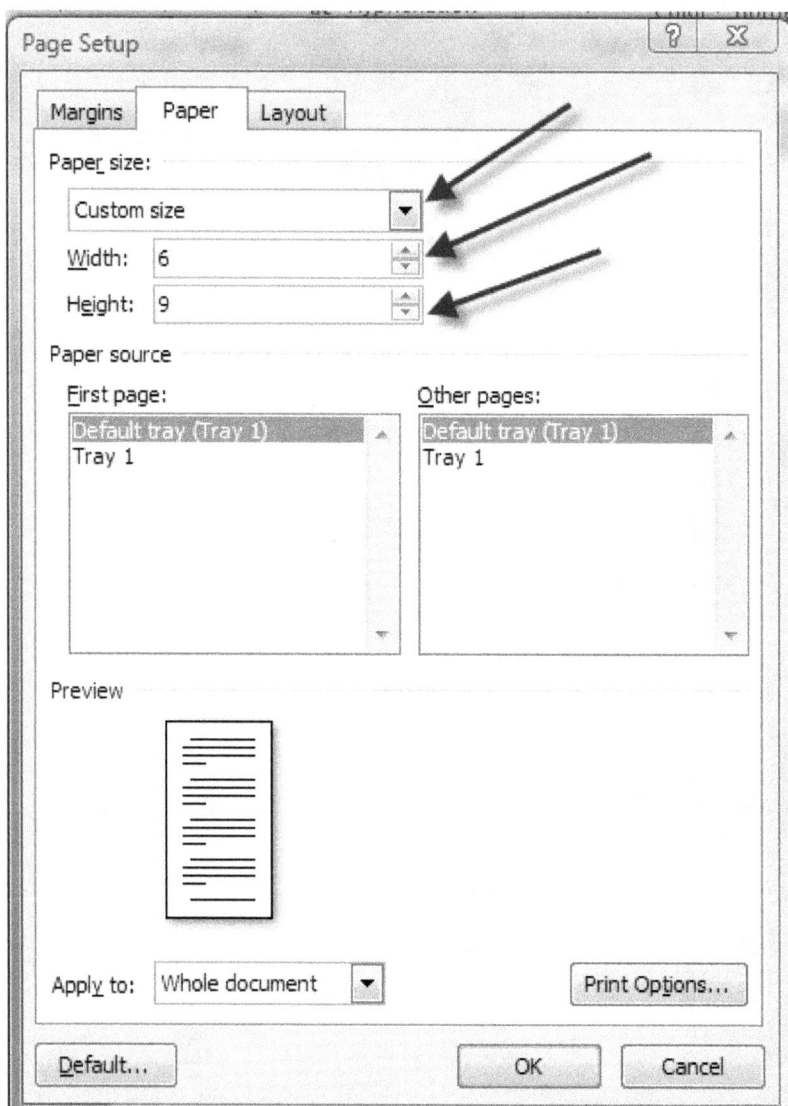

Select Custom Size to change the page size of your book. I selected 6" wide by 9" high for a 6x9 book. Make sure the "Whole Document" is still selected at the bottom of your screen.

Page Numbers

To add page numbers to your book, click the "Insert" tab on top of your Word 2007 screen.

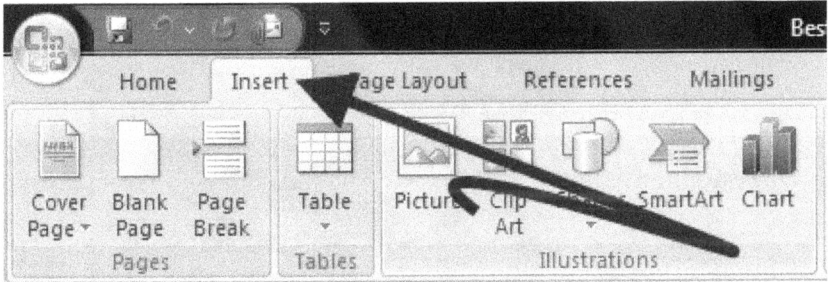

Click on the "Page Number" tab. Select "Top of Page" or "Bottom of Page" to set the location of your page numbers.

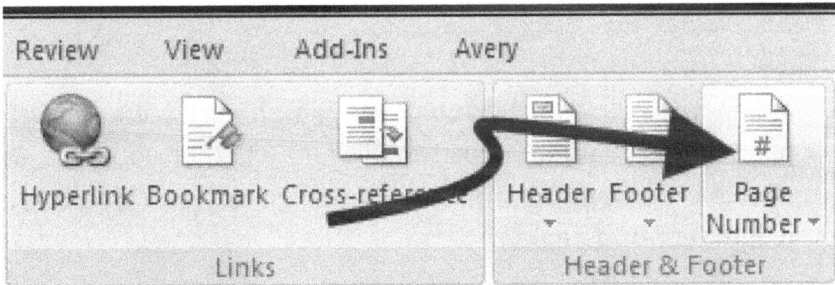

After you click on "Page Number, you will be prompted to select Top, Bottom, Margins, or Current position. You can place your page number to the right of your page, in the center, or on the left.

You can also choose the Format option.

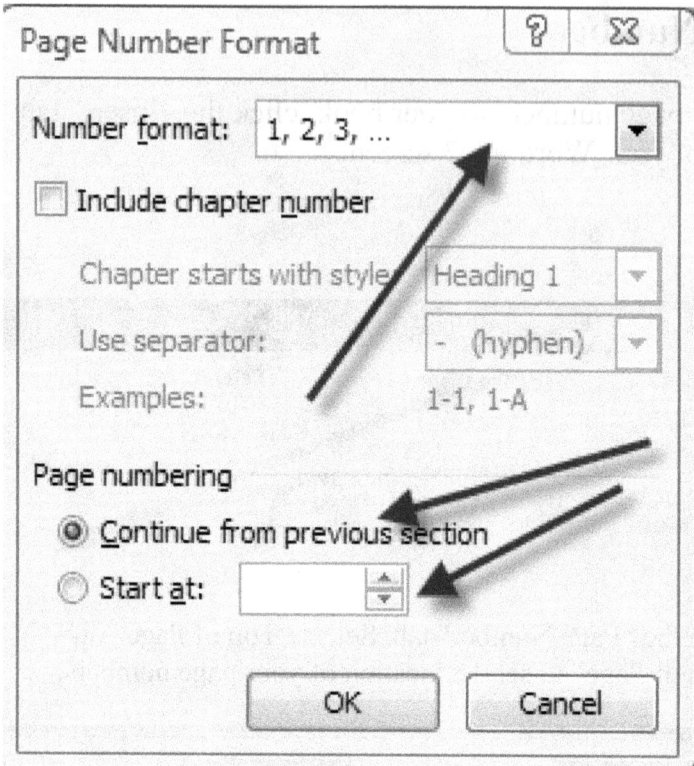

When you click on Format, you can choose your starting page number and number format, and whether you want to start the numbering from the previous section (if you are using Section Breaks).

These simple steps will help you set up your foundational layout for your book, Remember, the page you are viewing on the screen is exactly how your book will appear when printed.

> *Proofread carefully to see if you any words out. ~Author Unknown*

5

The Cover

The cover will sell the book, but a good cover won't make a bad book good.

You can address the cover two ways. The first is to create an image in your mind of how you want your cover to look and use that symbolism as a theme for your book.

An example is a photo of sprinters lined up at a starting line. Each chapter heading can be derived from a term used in track and field so the cover will parallel the theme of the book.

Or, you can finish your book and design a cover around a story element. Many bestsellers have a cover photo showing only one minor scene in the novel. A compelling, well-designed graphic image will draw shoppers to look at your book, and it really helps if your name is Jack Cavanaugh.

CreateSpace has a selection of free cover templates you can use to design your cover. Non-fiction books can easily get by with a cover that is simple, with bold colors and attractive cover text. If your book title is, *How To Make $1,000,000 in Ten Days*, a graphic of a million dollar bill on a flat background will probably be good enough. The title told the reader exactly what the book is about. If you have too many fancy graphics, the cover will take away from the title.

Fiction books warrant themselves to more colorful, detailed graphics. A simple way to create a cover is to use a photograph for the front and back panels. Select a photo (or take one yourself) that shows what the book is about.

For *Oakcreek Adventure*, I walked our local golf course and found a nice setting with a pond near the 13th green with a backdrop of tall trees. There were several buildings in the background but I easily hid those by pasting bushes over them using Photo Impact Pro.

The low trees to the left of "BY" are hiding the buildings. In full color, it's attractive and tells the reader that this is an adventure book about something that happened at Oakcreek. (see page 62)

The reader knows it is fiction, most likely for kids, and not too serious but will be an interesting book for kids to read. The back cover is the rest of the photo with more buildings removed by pasting in trees and branches. My short description on the back is covering a plain, brown mountain. Eventually I will change the cover to show two kids sailing across the pond on a rickety raft.

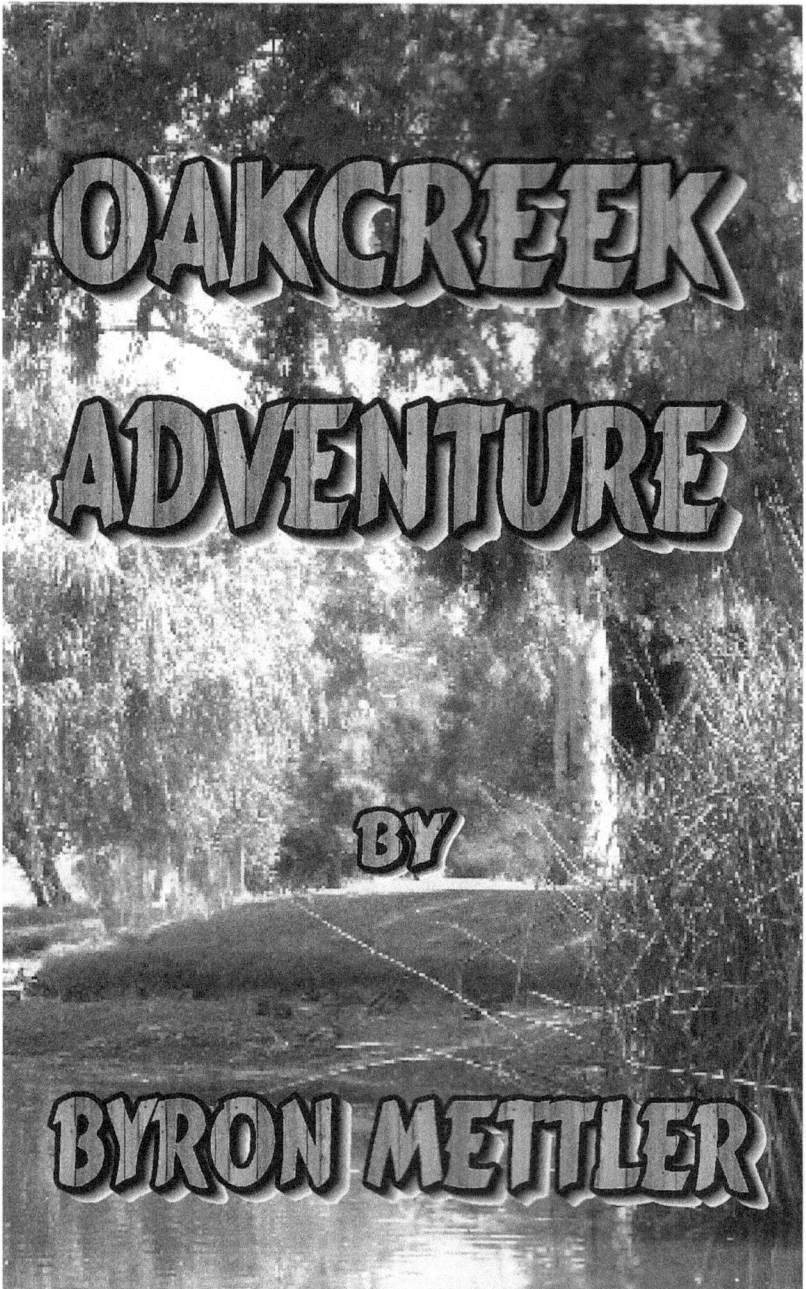

SUMMER SUN BROUGHT NEW ADVENTURES
EVERY DAY AS JIM AND RICK
EXPLORE THE MYSTERIOUS POND AT THE
END OF OAKCREEK RIVER.

FOLLOW THEIR ADVENTURES AS
THEY BUILD A RIVER RAFT,
FIND NEW CREATURES,
AND ENCOUNTER THRILLING
EXCITEMENT AT EVERY TURN!

a UNIKGIFTS publication

ISBN 978-1449509705

More on Software

I'm rather cheap so I purchased Printshop 22 to use on my desktop computer which has an XP operating system. I use Printshop Version 23 on my new laptop with Vista installed. After I purchased the laptop with Vista, I soon discovered that many XP programs would load but not work properly due to missing menu items. It took me days of frustration and several phone calls to the software reps to figure this problem out.

Web Easy gave me a free upgrade to use on my XP laptop just because they are nice people.

The purpose for your cover software is simple.

1-   You need a graphic program to make it look great.
2-   You need to save it to a PDF file.

You can spend a little or as much as you want to buy the software that works for you.

Printshop Hints

To create your cover in Printshop, select "Signs" as your page style. "Wide" as your page orientation and "11 x 17" as your page size.

This will give you an area 11 inches high and 17 inches wide for your front and back cover. This is large enough for all standard book covers. All elements for the front and back of your book are created as one file.

Find your vertical and horizontal center. Use the ruler on edge of the screen to measure the size of your cover. Add the spine width. The spine is the printed edge of the book that contains the author's name and book title. If you are not sure of the spine width, then allow 5/8 inch for the spine. You can change it later when you calculate your final page count.

As an example, a 6-inch by 9-inch book will have a total width of 12 5/8 inches. The height will be 9 inches.

When you place your cover art or cover background, make sure it bleeds over on all sides by at least ½ inch. This will give some tolerance when the printer cuts the book to size.

Artwork

If you are a born artist, you are already ahead of 98% of self-publishers because you can create your own designs and they will look great.

If you have five thumbs and plan to use art from other sources, be sure to look for copyright restrictions. I will peruse royalty photo sites to get ideas, but I'm still too cheap to pay the $500-$5,000 royalty fee to use the service. But I won't steal one either.

Many graphic programs you purchase include artwork files but may have restrictions for "personal use only." When you publish a book, you move from personal use to commercial use.

The software license may have an exception for a short run of books that only you and your family will buy, or for educational publications. Be sure to check with the program creator for legal use.

Layout

Standard cover sizes for Black and White books are.

Page Size	Page Count	Page Count	
White Paper or Cream Paper			
5 x 8 inches	24 - 828	24 - 740	*
5.06 x 7.81 inches	24 - 828	24 - 740	*
5.25 x 8 inches	24 - 828	24 - 740	*
5.5 x 8.5 inches	24 - 828	24 - 740	*
6 x 9 inches	24 - 828	24 - 740	*
6.14 x 9.21 inches	24 - 828	24 - 740	*
6.69 x 9.61 inches	24 - 828	24 - 740	
7 x 10 inches	24 - 828	24 - 740	
7.44 x 9.69 inches	24 - 828	24 - 740	*
7.5 x 9.25 inches	24 - 828	24 - 740	*
8 x 10 inches	24 - 440	24 - 400	*
8.25 x 6 inches	24 - 220	24 - 200	
8.25 x 8.25 inches	24 - 220	24 - 200	

Standard cover sizes for Full-Color books

Page Size	Page Count White Paper	
5 x 8 inches	24 - 250	
5.06 x 7.81 inches	24 - 250	
5.25 x 8 inches	24 - 250	
5.5 x 8.5 inches	24 – 250	*
6 x 9 inches	24 - 250	
6.14 x 9.21 inches	24 - 250	
6.69 x 9.61 inches	24 - 250	
7 x 10 inches	24 - 250	*
7.44 x 9.69 inches	24 - 250	
7.5 x 9.25 inches	24 - 250	
8 x 10 inches	24 – 250	*
8.25 x 6 inches	24 - 212	
8.25 x 8.25 inches	24 – 212	

* Industry Standard Required for Expanded Distribution Channel

Select the size you want for your book. You must use the Industry Standard trim size if you intend to use the Expanded Distribution Channel which will make your book available to more retailers at a discount.

.

CreateSpace tip

Distribution Channels <u>ISBN</u> <u>Trim Size</u> <u>Page Count</u>

Amazon.com Channel

Can have either your own ISBN or a CreateSpace-assigned ISBN Industry standard or custom trim size 24 or more pages.

eStore Channel

Can have either your own ISBN or a CreateSpace-assigned ISBN Industry standard or custom trim size 24 or more pages.

Expanded Distribution Channel

Distribution outlets available through the Expanded Distribution Channel

CreateSpace Direct Can have either your own ISBN or a CreateSpace-assigned ISBN Industry standard or custom trim size 24 or more pages.

Bookstores and Online Retailers Can have either your own ISBN* or a CreateSpace-assigned ISBN Must use an industry standard trim size** **Black & White:** 48 or more pages.

Full Color:
24 or more pages-
Libraries and Academic Institutions Must have a CreateSpace-assigned ISBN Industry standard or custom trim size 24 or more pages.

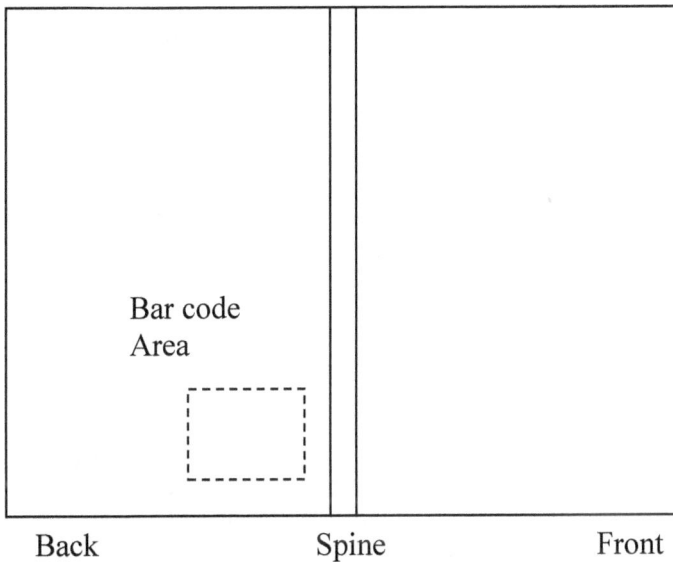

Back   Spine   Front

The Cover

Your book cover is the most visible part of your book and should be your best work. My experience with covers is that the cover should be good, or at least should not be horrible, but it doesn't have to a major work of art.

I did cover research and found that frequently published authors such as Stephen King often have twenty or thirty covers for the same title. Each cover is from a different publisher or a new edition or for a foreign audience; but all of them have a different look.

I believe that there are many good covers for each book.

The cover should say what the book is about, either with text or photo. The cover should be simple but eye appealing. The executive design decisions are up to you. You can hire an illustrator or graphic artist if you feel the need.

However, With CreateSpace you can change the cover and/or the entire content any time you want with no additional charge. You will need to purchase a proof copy (at your cost plus shipping) for approval before the changes go into production.

CreateSpace has a few simple rules for cover design.

Creating your cover file
https://www.createspace.com/Products/Book/#content3

Your cover must be a single PDF that includes the back cover, spine and front cover as one image.

You can submit your cover on any size page as long as the printable area is:

  * Measured exactly for your book's trim size, spine width, and at least .125" bleed
  * Centered horizontally and vertically

Minimum Cover Width: Bleed + Back Cover Trim Size + Spine Width + Front Cover Trim Size + Bleed

Minimum Cover Height: Bleed + Book Height Trim Size + Bleed

Safe Zone: Text and important images must be at least .25" inside the trim lines to ensure no essential elements are cut during the bookmaking process.

Bleed: Your cover's background must extend at least .125" beyond your final trim size to accommodate for cutting variance. Do not include any crop or registration marks in your artwork.

Barcode: When your title is printed, our system will place your ISBN barcode in a 2" by 1.2" white box in the lower right-hand corner of your book's back cover. Our standard trim size templates will show you exact barcode placement.

> **CreateSpace tip**
> How much space should I leave for my book cover's ISBN barcode if CreateSpace is placing the ISBN for me?
>
> The ISBN barcode will be in a white box 2" wide and 1.2" tall. The bottom of this ISBN barcode is located 1/4" up from the bottom trim line of the cover, and the right side of the ISBN barcode is located 1/4" to the left of the spine. Please ensure that you don't have any important images or text in the ISBN barcode location. You can also refer to our Artwork Templates for the exact size and position of the ISBN barcode

Images or text in the barcode location will be covered when the book is printed. Make sure you don't have any important elements where the barcode will be placed.

Spine Width and Variance

Every book will vary slightly when bound. For best results, avoid hard vertical separations between your cover panels and spine. Allow for at least a .125" variance of your spine on each side (for example, the text on a 1" spine should be no larger than .75" wide).

For books with a page count of less than 130 pages, we strongly recommend a blank spine. Blank spines are required for books with a page count of fewer than 100 pages.

Your spine width is calculated based on the number of pages in your book:

For black and white-interior books:

  * White paper: multiply your page count by 0.002252
  * Cream paper: multiply your page count by 0.0025

Example of spine width calculation for a 60-page black and white book printed on white paper
  60 x 0.002252 = 0.135" spine width
Page Count
108   x0.002252   =0.243216
125   x0.002252   =0.2815
150   x0.002252   =0.3378
175   x0.002252   =0.3941
200   x0.002252   =0.4504
225   x0.002252   =0.5067

250	x0.002252	=0.563
275	x0.002252	=0.6193
300	x0.002252	=0.6756
325	x0.002252	=0.7319
350	x0.002252	=0.7882
375	x0.002252	=0.8445
400	x0.002252	=0.9008

For color-interior books:

* Multiply your page count by 0.002347
Example of spine width calculation for a 60-page color book
60 x 0.002347 = 0.141" spine width

If you decide to design your own cover, you will need software you are comfortable using.

I use Print Shop Publisher Pro Deluxe 22 and 23 to design my covers.

Four Important Cover Elements

Bleed. Your background must run over on all four sides to allow cropping.
Text or photos. Keep hard elements 3/8" in from the outside edge of you cover for cropping.

Barcode. Allow a 2" x 1 1.2" space on the right bottom of the back cover for the barcode.

Back cover text. Tell the customer what the book is about in as few words as possible. If you have a review or expert recommendation, you can use that here. Remember, if you later want to change the cover text, perhaps you receive a great review later, you can always send in a new cover.

It is up to you as the designer to create an excellent cover for your book.

CreateSpace Cover Designer

You can bypass the software problems associated with the cover design and use the free Cover Designer on the CreateSpace website. Templates are available and there are some limitations, but it is a cheap and easy way to get a nice cover for your book.

CreateSpace tip

Can I change the positioning of words, pictures, and other elements on my Cover Creator cover?

The Cover Creator designs were professionally created in order to make the cover layout process as simple as possible. The placement and appearance of the design elements cannot be manipulated in any way.

> *A writer is somebody for whom writing is more difficult than it is for other people.* ~Thomas Mann, Essays of Three Decades, 1947

6

Uploading!

After you have written your book, completed a line edit, checked all of your spelling and grammar, cleaned up your layout, inserted the proper credits and legal jargon, and designed an eye-catching cover, you are ready to upload your book to CreateSpace.

Once you understand the process, the CreateSpace site is straightforward and the uploads are easy and fast.

Go to **www.createspace.com**

Click on Start Title For Free

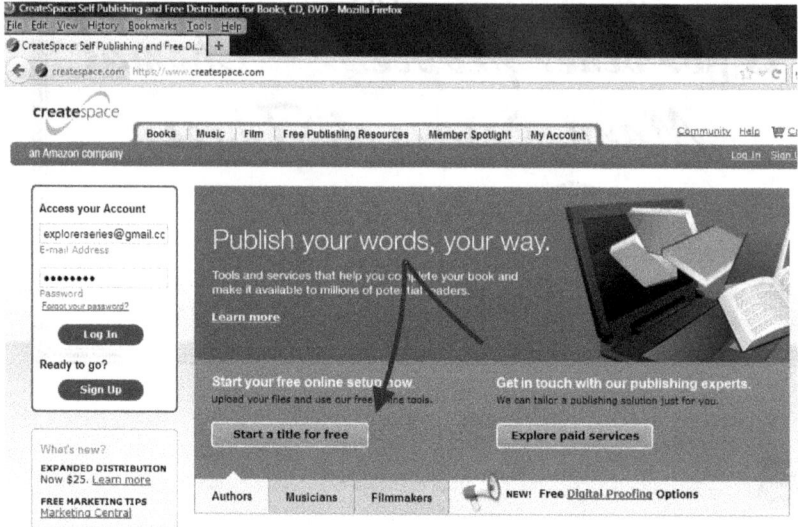

The CreateSpace home page gives you three options. Authors. Musicians. Filmmakers.

Before going further, click on My Account and set up your free account.

You need a PayPal account (at no cost) to have your royalty payments deposited directly to your account and you must provide your Social Security number for tax reporting purposes.

Then go back to the home page.
Click on Create

Start Your New Project

* Required

1 **Tell us the name of your project** *

Poor Old Willy

You can change your title at any time before you submit your project for review.

2 **Choose which type of project you want to start** *

| ⦿ **Paperback** | ○ Audio CD | ○ DVD |
| | ○ MP3 | ○ Video Download |

3 **Choose a setup process** *

| Guided | A step-by-step process with help along the way. | Get Started |
| Expert BETA | A streamlined single-page experience for those familiar with the process. | Get Started |

Title: The book title is the most important part of your book. Titles cannot be copyrighted so you can use any title you want. A sample title might be "Work Smart."

Click "Get Started' and move on to your book description.

CreateSpace tip

Description
This is where you tell your customers about the title. You have up to 1000 characters, or about 190 words.

This will send you to the **Title Information** page

Description: This is important.. Your description will be seen on the CreateSpace e-store site as well as on Amazon. This can be edited at any time but make sure you have the text correct before your final proof approval.

"How to accomplish more in a fraction of the time. *Working Smart* will teach you how to save time and money by focusing your best efforts on your most productive tasks. Over 100 experts contributed to this award winning edition of Working Smart to help you make your business a success."

Review the requested information and type your answers on a blank Word page. Check spelling and accuracy before pasting the information on CreateSpace.

Subtitle: "100 Ways to Make More Money While Working Less Hours."

Volume Number: If you have multiple volumes select which one here.

Click "Save and Continue" and enter your ISBN selection.

Click on "Information on ISBNs" for more information.

ISBN: This is the number and barcode on the back of every book. CreateSpace will give you a free ISBN number. Or, you can buy ISBN numbers for about $100 each or buy a block of 10 for about $250. If you want to be listed as the Book Publisher, you need to purchase your own ISBN number. I suggest using Bowker at www.bowkerlink.com.

Imprint Name: If you own your ISBN number enter the name of your publishing company. If you don't own your ISBN number, leave this blank. (Even if you use the free ISBN, you can still list your own publishing name on the back cover and on the copyright page of your book.)

BISAC Category: Select your book category.

I selected Free Createspace Assigned ISBN.

Next, you move on to your book Interior

Select Black and White, or Color interior.

Select your page Color,-Cream or White.

Select your Page Size, and if your book is finished and formatted as a pdf, you can Click "Upload Your Book file".

You will be prompted to search for your book file. Select "Browse" and locate the file to Upload.

Choose how you'd like to submit your interior:

◉ Upload your Book File

You can upload your work as a print-ready .pdf, .doc, .docx, or .rtf. Your page count will be detected and an automated print check will run once your upload is complete. You'll be able to see any issues online using the Interior Reviewer tool.

* **Required**

Interior File * [_____] [Browse]

The following formats are accepted: pdf,doc,docx,rtf

You do not have to upload the interior at this time. You can finish writing your book and upload at a later date.

After you complete your book setup, a Member Dashboard will automatically be created for you. The Member Dashboard is where you will access your book to complete or edit your information. You can also track your sales and and royalty amount.

Member Dashboard
Byron Mettler, Member ID 414195

Royalty Balance Details   Show: Total | June

	£0.00	€0.00
USD	GBP	EUR

Message Center ⚠ **29 alerts** ✉ **156 messages**

My Projects (Add New Title)

Sort By Recently Updated ▾
☐ Show subtitles and volume numbers

Title Name	Status	Jun Units			ID
Poor Old Willy	Incomplete	- June Royalties	Order Copies		3899082
Inspirations	Available	- June Royalties	Order Copies		3466945
52 Great Bible Object Lessons	Proof Review	- June Royalties	Order Copies		3449817
Self-Publishing With...	Available	- June Royalties	Order Copies		3449943
Things My Mother Taught Me	Proof Review	- June Royalties	Order Copies		3449258
Oakcreek Adventure	Available	- June Royalties	Order Copies		3399313
I Feel Like Writing Poetry	Proof Review	- June Royalties	Order Copies		3397286
Chandler	Available	- June Royalties	Order Copies		3394717
Sixteen Stories by John Howard...	Available	- June Royalties	Order Copies		3392483
Out of Darkness	Available	- June Royalties	Order Copies		3393420

To edit on the Member Dashboard, click on your book and screen will open showing your options.

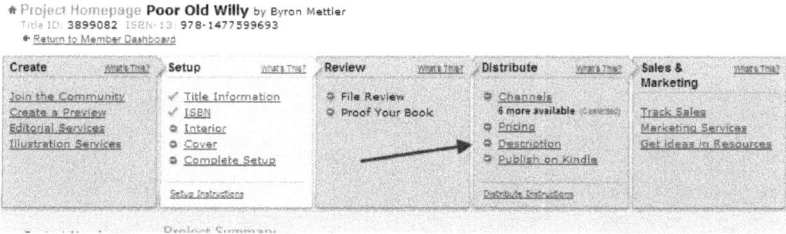

From this screen you can see the status of your project. You can also use this screen to enter more information.

On this page you can also elect your Sales Channels, enter or change your Book Price, edit your Description, and get help to publish your book on Kindle.

Select "Description" and a screen will open to let you enter the Author's biography and other pertinent information you may want to include.

Description How do I use this page?   ◄ Back   Next ►

Poor Old Willy
By Byron Mettler

Description *
What's this?

Maximum 4000 characters - 4000 characters remaining
Advanced users can use limited HTML instead of plain text to style
and format their description

BISAC Category *
What's this?   Choose...

→ **Enter a BISAC code**

Additional Information (optional)
Add more information about your book, including an author biography, book language, and more,
which will appear in certain sales channels.

Author Biography   Add ◄────
What's this?

Book Language   English   ▼
What's this?

Country of Publication Choose one   ▼
What's this?

Publication Date
What's this?

Search Keywords
What's this?

Contains Adult Content   ☐
What's this?

Large Print   ☐
What's this?

                                                    Save   Save & Continue

Skip to **Search Keywords:** This is important because this is how web surfers will find your book on the Internet. Go to:

https://adwords.google.com/select/KeywordTool External

and enter your book title to find keywords that match.

Contributors: If more than one person is responsible for your book enter their names.

Author Biography: Write a short narrative about yourself. Traditionally this is in third person.

When your have completed the Title page, click Save and Continue.

Uploading

This is the step you've been waiting for.

On your Project Homepage screen and select "Interior" and you will be directed to a page for uploading your book.

Click on "Upload you Book File" and a box opens so you can browse you computer to find the correct book file to upload.

Use the "Browse" button to search your files for the correct interior file. Click on your file and select Upload.

Select your file and click on "Upload."

The interior file size is limited to 100 MB, which shouldn't be a problem for you unless you have a full color book. My 438-page book is only 3 MB and my covers are usually about 10 MB. Covers files can be up to 40 MB.

When the file uploads, the pop-up box will change to a message informing you that your file was successfully uploaded. Repeat the same process with your book cover.

Upload Interior

Remember, with CreateSpace you can go back and make changes at any time at no cost to you. You can stop in the middle of your initial set up and come back later to finish it up.

Book interior checklist.

- ✓ Correct page size
- ✓ Interior paper color selected (White/Beige)
- ✓ Properly format headers
- ✓ Format page numbers
- ✓ Insert copyright information
- ✓ List your other publications
- ✓ Give credit to quoted texts
- ✓ Thank you page to those who helped you
- ✓ Index
- ✓ Chapter headings are consistent
- ✓ Fonts are consistent throughout
- ✓ Editing and spell check is complete
- ✓ Graphics are in the right place
- ✓ Fonts are imbedded
- ✓ File saved as a PDF
- ✓ Print out a page size copy and review for errors.

You are ready to upload!

Click on the "Upload Interior" which will give you a pop-up box. Search your computer for the correct file. Click upload and let 'er rip!

When complete, you will receive a message stating "Upload Successful."

Upload Cover

By now, you should be getting really good at the publishing business.

Go back to your Project Homepage screen and select "Cover" and you will be directed to a page for uploading your book.

Book cover checklist

- ✓ Correct cover size
- ✓ Adequate bleed
- ✓ Cover art complete
- ✓ Title block centered
- ✓ Back cover text edited and spell checked
- ✓ Spine text placed properly
- ✓ Room left for the bar code
- ✓ You publication company name on the back
- ✓ Author photo/bio
- ✓ Save as PDF

Your first upload is a proof copy so you will have time to make changes. I've kept one book in the proof stage for six months because I was waiting for my editor to complete the final edit.

Click "Upload PDF" in the book cover section and search for your cover file. Click on your cover file and watch it go off to your print house. CreateSpace will let you know when it is uploaded. If the transmission is disconnected, try again and continue until it successfully sends.

Submit For Publishing

After you've uploaded your files select "Submit for Publishing."
(If you forget to click on "Submit for Publishing," you will receive a reminder email.)

```
Thank you for uploading the Interior file
for your book, "52 Great Bible Object
Lessons," Book #3449817, on Apr 25 2010
PT. When you are ready for your files to
be reviewed, please be sure to click the
Submit for Publishing button that appears
at the bottom of your book's Review Setup
page.
```

Sales Channel Management

You are the publisher so it is up to you to set the price of your book. The sale management page will show you the minimum price you can set. This is based on the cost of the printing, plus the cut that Amazon will take.

I suggest you look at other similar books to determine the correct market price. You can always enter discount codes for friends, churches or bookstores to give them a special discount. Most retail outlets buy copies at 45% off list. Set your list price so that you can give a 50% discount when customers buy from your CreateSpace store, and you still make a royalty.

CreateSpace recently added an "Expanded Distribution Sales Channel" option. This option will provide a wider distribution to retail outlets and major stores. However, if you select Expanded Distribution your royalty will be reduced for books bought by major bookstores and CreateSpace will charge you $20 to make changes to your cover or interior.

You do not need to make a decision right now. Later, when you have your marketing plan in place, you can go to your Account page and select Expanded Distribution to increase your sales options.

Review Setup

The Review Setup screen gives you the opportunity to review and make changes to everything you've entered. Your first copy will be a proof so you have time to make changes before your book is ready for publication.

You have the option to review your entire book online and approve it for publication.
Remember to hit "Save and Continue" on each screen to move to the next step.

Email response

After you've finished all the steps, you will be notified that your files have been uploaded and will be reviewed by CreateSpace to confirm acceptable formatting. Once your files are successfully uploaded, you will receive an email confirming the upload

> Thank you for submitting your book, "Self-Publishing With CreateSpace," Book #3449943, on Apr 26 2010 PT. We will review your files and book information and notify you of the results via email shortly, typically within 24-48 hours.

Files Approved

Most of the books I have submitted were approved for order within 6 to 12 hours. CreateSpace will send you an email informing you when a proof copy is ready to order.

The correspondence will also inform you of possible problem areas you may want to address before ordering your proof copy. You can leave it as it is and order a proof for review, or upload corrected files and wait a day or so for the review.

The interior and cover files for Things My Mother Taught Me have been reviewed and are printable in their current state.

The ISBN and imprint name information entered for this title has not been verified at this stage. If there are any issues with the ISBN and imprint name entered for this title, you will be notified.

The interior file contains images that range from 116 to 214 DPI, which may appear blurry and pixelated in print. For optimal printing, we recommend all images be at least 300 DPI.

The interior file contains several pages with color images. Note that these images will print in black and white, as you have selected a black and white submission type.

The files submitted for this title contain text referencing Amazon.com.Â Please note that we will remove text and/or logos which reference Amazon.com.

You may upload new files or you may proceed with the publishing process using the current files.

If you would like to upload new files, you may wish to review the Submission Requirements, available at:
https://www.createspace.com/Products/Book/Submission.jsp

Ordering a Proof Copy

You can order multiple copies of your book for proofing and you can select two-day shipping if you are in a hurry.

You can also proof and approve your book online, or download a free pdf copy and review it on your computer.

Each proof copy has the word "Proof" stamped on the last page so you know it is not the final version. After ordering your proof copies, you will be sent an email to confirm your order.

I used second day shipping for my last book order and received my proof in 5 days. I ordered it on Monday and received it on Friday. It only took CreateSpace three days to print and package the book for shipping. That's pretty quick!

Standard shipping will take about two weeks depending on the size of your order. You should review your proof carefully to make sure you are satisfied with the results. If you want to make changes, you can upload a new cover or interior and order a new proof. There is no cost to you for uploading revised files.

Approve Proof

The last step to publish your book is to approve the proof. By now you have received your proof copy, reviewed the content and are satisfied with the final copy.

Your Member Dashboard on your CreateSpace account will now show an "Approve Proof" box. Click on "Approve Proof" and you will be sent to the order page.

Clicking Approve Proof will complete the process and you book is now ready for order. In a few days, you will see your book listed on Amazon with your bio and description exactly as you wrote it. But, you can always go back to make changes if you need to update the information.

| 1. Title Setup | 2. File Review | 3. Order Proof | 4. Print Ready |
| Complete | Complete | 1 of 2 complete | Incomplete |

Proof Review

| Order Proof | Proof Review |

Approve Proof

Title Information (Complete) Edit

Title ID   3449943
Title   Self-Publishing With CreateSpace

Congratulations! You are now a published author.

> *There are thousands of thoughts lying within a man that he does not know till he takes up the pen and writes. ~William Makepeace Thackeray*

7

How I Did It

Wrote Books - Became Frustrated - Self-Published Books.

I've been writing seriously for over eighteen years. I wrote my first book *Oakcreek Adventure* in 1994 but did not publish it until 2010.

I wrote *Chandler* in 1995 and pitched it to dozens of publishers and agents around the country. The best review

I received was "eminently publishable" but never was able to sell it. I published *Chandler* using CreateSpace in 2009. In 1997, I wrote *Speed Kills!,* the first book in the Police Explorer Series which was published through Publish America in 2007.

I have written articles for local papers, newsletters and magazines.

In 2009-10 I also published Sixteen *Stories by John Howard Ladd, I Feel Like Writing Poetry, Things my Mother Taught Me, Out of Darkness, Inspirations,* by Barbara McBride, *Oakcreek Adventure* and *The Best Book On Self-Publishing With CreateSpace.*

Sample Layout

Review the following examples to help you lay out your book pages.

The first page in your manuscript will be the Title Page.

Select the font you want for your title. Set the font size for the largest size that will fit on the page but still be in proportion to the rest of the text.

Place your name as the author in large font. If you want a sub-title, place that on this page also.

OUT OF DARKNESS

BY

BYRON METTLER

HE BROUGHT THEM OUT OF
DARKNESS... AND BRAKE THEIR
BANDS IN SUNDER

In MS Word, go to File. Select "Page Setup." Set the margins for the entire document.

Select "Mirror Margins."

Set the Inside Margin no less than .8. Much of this will be crowded out with the binding and if you make it narrow to save paper your book will be difficult to read.

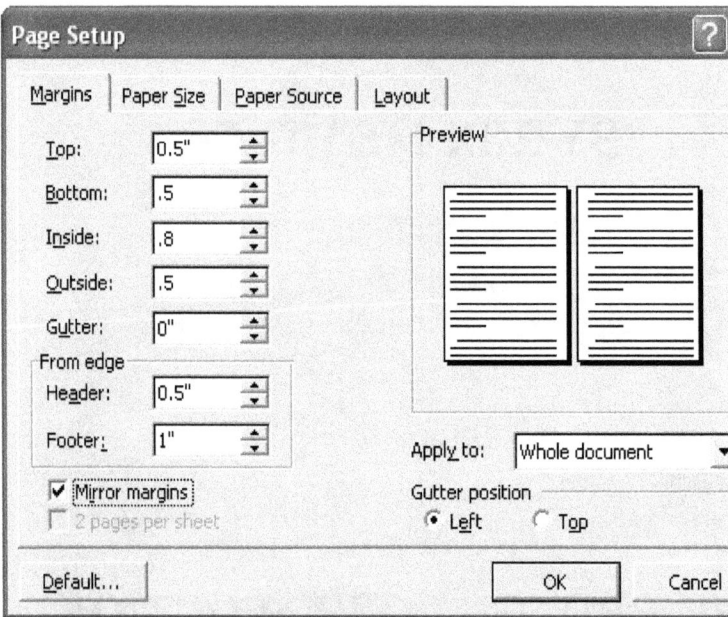

Page 2 is your copyright page.

This is also where you place any credit for borrowed works or references to real people. If you are using Bible translations in your book, list the information on this page.

There is no need to register a copyright for your book with the Library of Congress. For works published before March 1, 1989, a formal copyright notice was required to receive copyright law protections. In 1989 the law was changed. For works published after March 1, 1989, no copyright notice need be placed on the work in order for full copyright protection to apply. However you still should place the following notice on your work: Copyright © 2012 by Author's Name. All Rights Reserved.

I never pass up an opportunity for self-promotion and since I'm the publisher, I place my recently published books here.

My publishing company is **UNIKGIFTS Publishing Company** so I also list this on the second page just like the New York publishers.

All names are fictional. Some stories are based on actual police cases I was a part of.

The Meth Stories by Jimmy, Autumn, Edna, John and Barb are based on stories published on the Stories Of Meth website at http://www.kci.org. Used by permission.

First printing.

Email Byron at:
explorerseries@gmail.com

a UNIIKGIFTS publication

Byron's books:
Speed Kills! - 2007 winner of the Nancy Bayless Award
sixteen Stories by John Howard Ladd:
            Complied by Byron Mettler
Chandler
Things my Mother Taught Me
Oakcreek Adventure

Cover photo by Byron Mettler

Page 3 is your Thank You page.

THANKS to my loving wife Jeannie, for helping with the final edit and putting up with me while I spent countless hours keying in this story. The great title was her idea.

Thanks Brenna, for bringing Pedro to the story. His character filled in a much-needed aspect.

I owe the San Diego Christian Writers Guild and the Ramona Critique Group special thanks for providing guidance and encouragement to continue writing.

Many of the good parts in the book are due to suggestions from Pete Zindler, Edna Hill, Sharon Cargo and Gail Prout who took the time to read each line and provide corrective criticism.

A sad thanks to the drug users and lost souls whose stories added realism to this novel. I hope some of you have found your way.

Thanks to Jesus. Without you, I'm just another lost soul searching for truth.

Thanks Mom and Dad. You've always encouraged me.

Thanks to "Faces of Meth" for posting the despondent photos of meth users. Search their site and I'll bet you'll find pictures of Brett Baker, Crank, Lester and Pamela at http://www.facesofmeth.us/

Special thanks to Darrell Wehmeier at "Meth Stories" for allowing me to use five true stories of meth addiction in Chapter 7. You can read more meth stories at http://www.kci.org.

Page 4 is blank

Page 5 is the same as the Title Page without the author's credit.

OUT OF

DARKNESS

Book Two in the

Police Explorer Series

Page 6 is blank

Page 7 is your first chapter or preface. You can also include any front matter you want to include. I inserted the Miranda Warning.

<u>Miranda Warning</u>

You have the right to remain silent.

Anything you say can be used against you and will be used against you in a court of law.

You have the right to talk with an attorney and to have an attorney present during questioning.

If you cannot afford an attorney, one will be appointed free of charge before and during questioning.

Do you understand each of these rights I have explained to you?

With these rights in mind, do you wish to talk to me now?

Yes or no?

Page 8 is blank

Page 9 is the table of contents. This is not necessary for novels unless you want to add chapter titles. Many novels may contain dozens of chapters and it would be cumbersome to create a name for each chapter.

All non-fiction books should have a table of contents and often include section titles.

TABLE OF CONTENTS

Page10 is blank.

Page 11 is the start of the first chapter.

I prefer to start my chapters on an odd page. It allows the reader to start each chapter reading on the right page.

THE DARK SIDE

Prologue

"Ready?" Agent Crawford asked.

"Ready when you are," Agent Wilson, a Narcotics and Gang Task Force member whispered. Behind him stood seven drug agents wearing black tactical masks and jump suits with bright yellow NGTF on the back. Each officer carried a 10mm Glock semi-automatic handgun strapped to their hip in a paddle holster.

The sky loomed midnight black over the small white house with the white picket fence. The sweet aroma of fresh baked cookies once greeted visitors at the door, but now the bitter chemical odor of methamphetamine seeped out through the clapboard siding. It looked just like grandma's house, but grandma didn't live here anymore. The home was a drug house, rented by dealers to cook up methamphetamine.

"Is anyone inside?" Agent Wilson asked.

So far, you haven't seen a header at the top of the page or page numbers at the bottom. Start your header and page numbers after the front matter.

Microsoft Word has a function to install page headers and page numbers in your document. You can also use Section Breaks to change the header for each chapter.

My software has a bug in it so I was unable to set the section breaks properly. Since it's my book and I'm the publisher, I made an executive decision to work around the problem.

On pages 1-10, I blocked out the header at the top and page number at the bottom by inserting a small text box over each item. I then selected No Line and a "white" text box to cover the wording on the header and the page number.

It's okay to cut corners if you can get away with it. It's your book.

OUT OF DARKNESS

"Brett Baker. He lives here with his girlfriend Pamela Sawyer. Their latest batch of Meth is drying and they are going to cut it and bag it in the morning."

"Let's go!" Crawford signaled.

Two agents went to the rear to block escape from the back door. One went to the right side of the house and one to the left. The remaining agents ran toward the front door. The group moved in unison like a tactical brigade of well-trained experts. The lead agent carried a Blackhawk 32 inch 10 lb Thundersledge. He ran up the steps to the front door and yelled,

"Police Officers! We have a warrant! Open the door!"

He cocked both arms back to a full swing and piled the weight of the Thundersledge against the deadbolt, splintering the door jam to bits. The door burst open with a crash and three agents stormed into the house pointing their Glock handguns high and low.

"Cops!" A man's voice shouted from the bedroom. Shattering glass erupted through the bedroom window.

The agent at the side heard the smashing glass and turned to see Brett Baker soaring toward him through the air surrounded by chips of broken glass. Brett crashed into the officer and knocked him to the ground.

"Stop," the officer yelled and grabbed for Brett's arm. Brett twisted and pulled away. He rolled one more time, sprung to his feet and bounded over the white picket fence in the front yard. The officer jumped to his feet and ran after him holding his Glock in one hand and calling for assistance on his radio with the other. He hurdled the picket fence and chased him down the sidewalk.

Seconds later, Pamela Sawyer jumped out of the same broken window, she lost one shoe, fell to the ground and rolled across the grass. She crab-crawled to the edge of

The following pages include the text for your book. You can insert pictures, graphics, artwork, and change fonts as needed to make the book more appealing.

You can be as creative as your imagination allows because this is your book. Anything is acceptable, as long as it fits the expectations of your intended audience.

Let your imagination soar and create the book of your dreams. No limits!

> *The words of a man's mouth are as deep waters, and the wellspring of wisdom as a flowing brook.*
> *Proverbs 18:4*

8

Marketing- Now you got it - Time to sell it

Family and Friends

Friends and family members can be a great a cheerleading section for your premier book. At first, they'll think you're great, later believe you're crazy, then they will sit back and watch to see if you *really* have what it takes to finish your book. After a while, you will be ignored and treated like the eccentric hermit in the family who spends all day clicking away at a keyboard.

And when you finally publish your book, a faithful few will step up and buy a full-price copy from Amazon or Barnes and Noble. If you sell one hundred books to your loyal followers, you'll be as successful as 99% of your fellow self-publishers who've just published their first book.

Book Signings

Book signings, or author signings as experienced authors like to call them, are an excellent way to get your name out in the community and get real-life feedback from your fans. I like to sign with two or three authors because the varied genre brings in all kinds of people.

Often times, a single visitor will go down the line and buy a book from each author. People enjoy meeting real authors and love to have you sign a dedication to a special person in their life.

Be creative. Sign books at coffee shops, homeschool groups, bookstores, county fairs, libraries, churches, Kiwanis clubs, boys and girls clubs and anywhere people meet or shop.

Webpage

Yes.

If you are serious about self-publishing and selling your book you must have a sales outlet and you must have a platform. Your website is the correct foundation for both.

Your Internet presence will be as large as you want to make it. If nothing else, build or buy a website with YOUR NAME.COM on it and offer your books for sale. Last year I bought byronmettler.com just so I could own the rights to it. After all, what if I get famous overnight and someone else buys my name just so they can sell it to me for a lot of money. Well, it could happen.

Royalty Tip

When you market your book, always direct your customers to your book-specific CreateSpace eStore web address. You will receive 20% more royalty if they buy direct from your e-store at CreateSpace.

E-books

Here's a secret. Today, right now, in the next ten minutes, you can email your book to Amazon/Kindle and have your Kindle e-book listed on Amazon for sale at no cost to you. You set the price and you keep all the royalties.

Kindle Tip from David Carnoy on cnet news

- The author or publisher-supplied list price must be between $2.99 and $9.99.
- This list price must be at least 20 percent below the lowest physical list price for the physical book.
- The title is made available for sale in all geographies for which the author or publisher has rights.
- The title will be included in a broad set of features in the Kindle Store, such as text-to-speech. This list of features will grow over time as Amazon continues to add more functionality to Kindle and the Kindle Store.
- Under this royalty option, books must be offered at or below price parity with the competition, including physical book prices. Amazon will provide tools to automate that process, and the 70 percent royalty will be calculated off the sales price.
- The 70 percent royalty option is for in-copyright works and is unavailable for works published before 1923 (aka public-domain books). At launch, the 70 percent royalty option will only be available for books sold in the United States.

Platform

I used to think of a platform as a table with multiple legs but now I see it as a bundle of colored balloons. To float in the air I either need one giant balloon or a whole bunch of little ones to defy the laws of gravity and get me on my way. An author's platform works the same way. The more balloons you hold in your hand, the better takeoff potential you have.

Key Platform tips

- ➤ Become an author of books or articles. Title your books, audio recordings and reports to explain your expertise. Use powerful key words.
- ➤ Any media experience. Local or national as a commenting expert.
  Did you built a better mousetrap? Did you make something new or better for your industry?
- ➤ Do you have endorsements or testimonials from industry leaders? Just a passing comment is okay. Thank them and ask if you can quote them. You are borrowing from their platform.
- ➤ Did your book receive awards or been a best seller? An award is simply group of people saying that your book is good.
- ➤ Build a strong community. Someone they will follow, admire and respect. Start a newsletter, Facebook page, Twitter account or blog.
- ➤ Lead a discussion group on the web. How many people want to hear what you have to say? Do not oversell your product. People are sick of marketers trying to push their way into a sale.
- ➤ This is the last platform spoke. What are your credentials? Certifications? Degrees? There are a lot of pretend experts out there. From what perspective are you presenting yourself?
- ➤ Listen to the 18 platform steps at:
http://instantteleseminar.com/?eventid=1759809

Selling Your Book

All marketing is about selling. Your marketing plan may include setting up a webpage, creating a blog, writing articles, speaking at local organizations, or joining a writers critique group.

You may have in your head the next, best, greatest novel ever written. You might even get all the words down on paper and use this book to self-publish your work. Soon, you will be up on Amazon and anyone of the six billion people living on this planet can buy your book. I'll bet you will even give them a discount if they ask for it.

But without marketing, your potential best seller will sit in the archives of the electronic storage world known only to the few in your direct circle of friends.

I hope you follow the trend of *The Shack* and become the surprise best seller of 2011. Use all your networking skills and marketing genius to tell as many people as you can about your outstanding new book. You must believe in yourself when no one else will.

9

20 Reasons Why You Should Self-Publish

1. The Next Big Thing
2. It's Cheaper Than You Think.
3. The Control Freak Inside - You Are In Control
4. You're The Best Agent In The World (For Your Product)
5. Your Expertise
6. Time Is On Your Side-
7. Your Marketing Plan Will Be Better Than
You Get From a Big Publishing House
8. More Royalty
9. Your Launching Pad
10. Fulfill Your Dream
11. It's Good For Your Brain
12. Leave a legacy
13. Tell The World What You Think –
Your Book Could Change The Future
14. Your Business Partners
15. Earn Residual Income
16. Only You Can Write Your Book
17. Therapy - Because You Can't Help Yourself
18. More Options Than Ever Before
19. The World Has Changed
20. Fun, Excitement and Adventure

1.

The Next Big Thing

Catch the wave on the newest trend in publishing.

BOWKER STATISTICS 2009: NON-TRADITIONAL MEANS NOW THE MAJORITY PATH FOR AUTHORS
by Editor on Wednesday, April 14, 2010

"The latest 2009 statistical report released by R.R. Bowker today is a real eye-opener. The total amount of titles produced last year was 1,052,803, and significantly, 764,448 of that overall figure came from what Bowker describe as non-traditional channels – a mix of micro-publishers, self-publishers and reprints of public domain titles.
In simple terms, 2010 will see non-traditional produced titles outstrip traditional titles by three to one—something that would have been considered mind-blowing three or four years ago. CreateSpace just passed their 2 million mark."

CHARLESTON, S.C. – May 24, 2010 –"From major publishing houses to independent authors, more and more people are able to reach broad audiences through the CreateSpace platform. CreateSpace, part of the Amazon.com, Inc. (NASDAQ: AMZN) group of companies, today announced an exciting milestone: more than 2 million book, DVD and CD titles have now been made available through the innovative full-service and do-it-yourself creative platform. These titles are made on-demand when customers order them and are continuously available on Amazon.com and other channels. With the recent launch of its Expanded Distribution Channel, a strong member community and a comprehensive suite of free tools and fee-based services, CreateSpace provides the most comprehensive solution for content owners who want to distribute their books, DVDs and CDs without inventory."

6/27/10

http://windblownmedia.com/advice-to-authors.html
"Windblown Media is not currently accepting any unsolicited manuscripts. We would however, like to offer some tips and advice for authors and artists looking to be published.

Advice for Authors

The publishers here at Windblown Media understand the frustrations and concerns of writers and artists looking to publish their work. The publishing industry is in great flux right now and it is harder than ever for a new writer to attract their attention. Fortunately, though, we are in a transitioning time that has allowed the Internet to become the acquisitions editor for the publishing industry. Never before have writers had such options to inexpensively put their ideas before the public and let their audience grow organically. If you can't find an audience for your passions and content on the web, a publisher is not going to be able to find it for you.

So let me encourage you to move ahead on your own. Don't wait for a publisher. Hopefully what The Shack demonstrated is that just about anyone can put a book out there in this viral world and it will find its audience in time. Today, especially with new authors, it is the author that sells their own works through the contacts God has given them and the range of their own influence. We can help in that process, but we cannot be a substitute for it. Books sales and reputations best grow organically, rather than through the artificial hype of press releases and interviews."

2.

It's Cheaper Than You Think.

Nothing. Yes, that's right. You don't have to pay any upfront costs to publish your next book.

This will shock you. Nada. That's right, you can hire a world renowned publishing house to print your next book for absolutely nothing. All you pay for is the cost of the finished book and the shipping of about $3.60 for a single book. Order more copies and you shipping cost per book will be substantially less. A recent book I published cost me $2.15 plus shipping.

How do they do it so cheap? I don't have a clue. Volume, I suppose.

I published my first book using Publish America and received an advance of $1 for my finished manuscript. They provided some editing and bound it nicely with an interesting cover. I later discovered I was saddled with trying to sell my 126-page, soft cover, young-adult fiction book for a list price of $19.95. Copies I purchased as the author were $12.96 plus shipping. I later bought some discounted copies for about $4.50 but the shipping was $3.99 per book, so that is still about $8.50 per book. I have two boxes of them in my closet if you know a kid who wants to read a great police action story!

The last box of books I published with CreateSpace cost me less than $3.00 per book, including delivery to my door. That's cheaper than a Hallmark greeting card.

3

The Control Freak Inside - You Are In Control

The traditional publishing contracts give total control of your book to the publisher and leave you with little to do except write a great book and then twist the storyline to meet the publisher's view of market trends.

I know an author friend who wrote an outstanding military thriller and was offered a contract from a large publishing house- if he agreed to make some changes. The action packed story took place on a navy ship in the middle of the Mediterranean Sea. The publisher wanted more romance and asked the author to include a few love scenes to spice it up. He didn't believe it to be an integral part of the story and refused to make the changes to make the publisher happy. He went forward to self-publish his book which won numerous awards and was later offered a film option.

As a self-publisher, you are in total control of your work and your have total freedom to make it your best work. You are the author, agent, layout expert and publisher, so you are responsible for your book's content and design.

Wow. That's a lot of responsibility for one person. Yes, but that's why you partner with experts in the field who are there to help you become successful. Other authors have spent tireless hours researching all aspects of the publishing industry to compile books on subjects you don't have time to research. You can use CreateSpace, or any Print on-Demand publisher to get a great finished book for you to market.

Be in charge and get out in front with the best book you can create. Be the boss!

4.

You're The Best Agent In The World (For Your Product)

For sixteen years I've quarried agents and publishers hoping to get my breakout novel published and become a surprise bestseller. Sending out queries is sort of like buying lottery tickets. You hope that one day you'll get the attention of a power broker who will take you under his or her wings and send you sailing into sudden success.

Real life doesn't work that way. Agents are looking for a sure thing. Publishers are looking for a guaranteed return on their investment of $30,000 to $50,000 spent on each book.

Are you so sure of your writing ability that you are willing to spend $50,000 to publish your book? Most of us will say no because new products always have a risk of failure. You may have in your hands the best book ever written. But two years from now, your information could be dated or another author will produce a work that is the new "Best Book Ever Written."

As a self-publisher, you are no longer dependent on an agent taking up your cause because you are in charge of your success. For a moment, put down your writers cap and pretend you are an agent. Pick up your manuscript, look at it through an agent's eye, and ask yourself, why you, the agent, would take up this authors cause? And, if you were willing to take it on, how would you sell the finished product? Then, take off your agent hat and put on the publishers visor. Why would you buy this book and what steps would to take to market it?

I don't doubt that you have a great book in mind, but you need to take an honest look at the finished product and make good business decisions. Of course, many authors will publish a book for a limited market expecting nominal sales, and that's okay as long as it's part of their business plan.

5.

Your Expertise

No one knows more about your book than you. You are an expert in your field. Your unique life experiences qualify you as the only person who can write your story.

That, in itself, makes you an expert. Dig into your past and find the diamonds in your life that will make your book great. All of us have something to say. How you say it will determine if others want to read your story. I never thought it possible to write an interesting book about a golf game. Golf, although a fun sport, is as boring to watch as watching bread rise. Hit the ball, watch it roll-it stops-hit it again. Repeat for eighteen holes.

But when I read *The Fast Green* I realized that a good writer will make any subject entertaining. The book adds drama, intrigue, suspense, betrayal, mystery, murder and a love story all wrapped up in eighteen holes of golf on an aging golf course in the middle of the desert.

The writer knew lot about the sport and wrote an entertaining story about golf, wrapped around a backdrop of mystery and drama. Make whatever you write an interesting story no matter what the subject matter. Your expertise will only work if you are a good story teller. That applies to fiction and non-fiction alike.

6.
Time Is On Your Side-

Traditional publishers take18 months to publish book.

Right now, this moment, you can upload your finished manuscript to Scribd or Kindle and become a published eBook author in one hour. Your book will be listed and available for the international market and you can start selling instantly. Never before, have we had so many sales options and it has never been easier to sell products.

You can search for "Lawn Chairs" in your browser and in seconds, you will be direct to a dozen sites that sell lawn chairs. In a minute you scroll through, click the site you want, select your favorite chair and have it delivered to your door in days.

If you decide to use CreateSpace or some other on-demand publisher, you can upload your book and have a finished product up on the web in less than 30 days for the entire world to buy. People love to buy on the web. It's easy. You save gas and time and consumer confidence has given Internet purchases respectability. Amazon media purchases have skyrocketed to almost $7 billion in 2009 and still rising. Media sales in the first quarter of 2012 had already hit $4.71 Billion.

Let's pretend you actually DID write the greatest book ever written and you want to get it published as soon as possible using traditional means. First, you prepare a proposal. Second, you attend writers conferences and pitch your proposal to a few agents who may be interested. Once you hook an agent, you mail or email them a complete proposal.

According to "Guide to Literary Agents, you will wait for weeks or months for a response. Most agents I queried take several months to return a reply. Okay, so let's say you hooked one and now you're ready to sell your book to the highest bidder. But next you have to finish your manuscript; including the editing and spell check and create a sure-thing proposal for the publisher to read. After that, your agent will mine his email list to find the right publisher for your book.

Now the agent goes to work and tries to lasso a publisher. Weeks, months go by and finally the agent is contact by an interested publisher. Time passes- and you finally have a signed contract giving the publisher full rights to your book for three years in return for 8% royalty based on the price the publisher sells the book to distributors. And don't forget to give your agent 15% of your royalty.

Twelve to eighteen months later, your book is published and sitting on Amazon offered for sale on the worldwide market. Two years have passed from proposal to market and you've just started your marketing plan.

Exactly where you would be if you had self-published two years earlier.

7.

Your Marketing Plan Will Be Better Than You Get From a Big Publishing House

Big publishers rarely put big bucks into marketing and will only do so if they have a sure thing in hand. If you are a recently impeached president or have just discovered you are the long lost Howard Hughes heir, you may get marketing money in your contract. But often, the cash spent on marketing will be paid back out of the author's royalty at a later day.

Marketing is what you make it. Mega preachers are instant marketers because they have thousands of buyers waiting for their next book. That's not a bad thing, it is just a fact. If you are already a famous entertainer, or TV personality, you may have a ready audience waiting to buy your book.

No one can market your book better than you. You believe in your product and are obnoxiously enthusiastic about your work. (You betcha') Excitement about your book starts with you. Your initial sales pitch about your book should be rehearsed, planned, practiced and sincere. You cannot hire and pay for more effective marketing.

8.
More Royalty

You will receive 700% to 1,000% more royalty by self publishing with CreateSpace than you would receive with traditional publishers. That is based on the $1.00 you may receive for a traditionally published book compared to the $7.00 or more for each self-published book sold.

Selling at full price through your CreateSpace eStore.

$13.99   Selling price -265 page book

Royalty Calculator*
Use the royalty calculator to figure out how much you'll make every time your book is manufactured.

Print Options

Interior Type	Black and White ▼	Number of Pages	265
Trim Size	5" x 8" ▼		

List Price	Channel	Royalty
	Amazon.com	**$4.35**
USD $ 13.99 Calculate	eStore	**$7.15**
	Expanded Distribution	**$1.55**
☑ Yes, suggest GBP price based on the U.S. price	**Amazon Europe** For books printed in Great Britain	**£2.05**
GBP £ 9.02 Calculate		
☑ Yes, suggest EUR price based on the U.S. price	**Amazon Europe** For books printed in continental Europe	**€2.95**
EUR € 11.24 Calculate		

* Figures generated by this tool are for estimation purposes only. Your actual royalty will be calculated when you set up your book.

Selling at full price with a traditional publisher

$13.99   Selling price - 265 page book
-12.87   Publisher take
- .17   Agents share
.95   My royalty

The last time I checked, more money per book equals a greater profit. If you can charge more for your books, your profit is even greater.

$21.95   Selling price - 450 page book.

$11.31   Your eStore   Royalty
$6.92   Your Amazon Royalty
$2.53   Your Expanded Distribution Royalty

9.
Your Launching Pad

Your first book can send you into the stratosphere of success.

Recently I looked up the author page for William P. Young and saw this message on his "Shack News" page.

"Sorry, the author has been too overwhelmed to keep up with this page. For all the latest news on The Shack please go to Windblown Media's website. The book will soon be appearing in more than 30 languages around the world and in audio versions in many countries as well. Thanks for all your interest and support."

William Young wrote an outstanding book, became an overnight success and went on to pursue greater ventures. As of May 2010, The Shack had over 10 million copies in print, and had been at number 1 on the New York Times best seller list for 70 weeks. His book was self-published three years ago and still ranks #139 on the Amazon Bestseller Rank.

Think of your first book as a business card. When you present yourself to others with a stapled manuscript printed on 8 ½" x 11" paper you are a would-be-author. But when you hand your friend a well-manufactured, bound copy with an interesting, vibrant cover, you become a credible author. Your first book may not be your best book, but if you have an author's heart beating inside you, it won't be your last book.

10.
Fulfill Your Dream

Your dream has to be large enough, strong enough, and big enough to carry you through from the first word to the final edit. Dream your dream and bring your dream to realty. You have a book locked away in your head waiting to come out and become stamped on paper for all to see. It is a dream made real.

It doesn't matter if it's a book of poetry, a collection of short stories or a weird science fiction novel you created on a dark and stormy night. This is your story and will soon be your book. I've spent many, many days and weeks punching alone on a keyboard struggling to stamp out just the right collection of words with a unique inflection that will bring a tear to the reader's eye. Occasionally, I get it right.

Working alone, I'm often lost in my world of characters and action as the real world carries on around me in a Time Machine fast actions sequence. Hours later, I look up, and discovered the sun has set, the dishes are put away and the house dark and quiet with everyone tucked safely in their beds.

The process of writing is the dream. The final product is the icing on the cake. The only thing I like more than a finished book is the prospect of starting the next one.

11.
It's Good For Your Brain

Getting old is hard. All the health gurus say that to stay young, you need to keep your brain active. Fighting with your computer to get out 40,000 words in some sort of order is a brain workout. If, for no other reason, write something because it's good for you.

Writing has a way of breaking a lot of bad habits, except maybe coffee drinking. You won't waste your time watching TV sitcom re-runs or searching the movie channels for a good movie. (There aren't any)

It's near impossible to put out good prose when you're under the influence of anything. The stories about Hemmingway drinking whiskey and publishing bestsellers I believe was propagated to portray his image of an eccentric writer, living out a dream of writing, fishing in Key West and drinking. He was actually a troubled man plagued with many demons who finally committed suicide in 1961.

Keep your thoughts pure and your mind active. Writing is guaranteed to take care of at least one of those.

12.
Leave a Legacy

Do you have a story to tell your grandkids? How will they hear it, if you leave before writing it down?

Each generation is blessed with its own version of life. My parents were blessed with a litany of American colloquiums. Those unique phrases and humorous examples are lost to the new generation. Families today rarely read mother goose rhythms, Peter Cottontail or A Child's Own Book of Verse

A birdie with a yellow bill
Hopped upon the window-sill;
Cocked his shining eye, and said,
"Ain't you 'shamed, you sleepy-head?"
—ROBERT LOUIS STEVENSON.

Growing up in the 60's, we coined the phrases, Out-a Sight, Groovy, Boss, What a Bummer, Dork, Drag and Dude. I wonder if my grandkids will ever know the history behind those phrases? Now is the time for you to tell your story to future generations.

13.
Tell The World What You Think - Your Book Could Change The Future

We all have opinions, but I like mine the best. Give me an hour and I'll tell you all about it.

Books that changed the world. Luther's Ninety-Five Theses, The Meaning of Relativity, Fifth Edition: Including the Relativistic Theory of the Non-Symmetric Field by Albert Einstein, Magna Carta: Second Edition by J.C. Holt, The Federalist Papers by Alexander Hamilton, Anne Frank - The Diary of a Young Girl.

Each of these books started with an idea, a story, or a conversation that grew into a lesson learned, that changed the world. Every book starts with a first line.

"Once upon a time…" add your story to the line.

14.
Your Business Partners

Amazon, CreateSpace, Google, Microsoft

When you become a publisher, you are partnering with the most successful corporations on this planet.

Microsoft needs you to use their software to write your book so you can send it to CreateSpace who needs your publication which you will sell on Amazon which uses Google to find customers.

They are all working for you and need your book to stay in business.

15.
Earn Residual Income

Many prominent authors make more money from residuals, such as speaking and teaching gigs, than they do from selling books. The royalty return on books is so low, and the expense of travel and support is so high that even successful authors need a second income to pay the bills.

Teaching, consulting, ghost writing, book editing and speaking at seminars are some ways you can make money with your new book. A finished book adds credibility and will open doors for you as you pursue your vision of becoming a winning author.

Spin-offs and excerpts from your book will continue to bring in income as you take portions of your book and re-brand them as magazine articles, web downloads, and updated editions.

Your book will be listed indefinitely on the web, and you will soon discover opportunities you never expected.

16.
Only You Can Write Your Book

You have a unique idea.

The world will be a better place, because you took your unique and very special idea and brought those thoughts to life on the pages of your book. Only you can write your story. It is exclusive to you.

A few years ago, I met with a publisher who was interested in one of my novels. We had a discussion about market trends and tried to project the next bestseller idea. He told me his company had just published a string of dragons and sorcery novels which had saturated the market, so they were looking for something new. This inside knowledge gave me a thrill because my finished action-packed novel had nothing to do with dungeons and dragons.

I sent my manuscript to his office and waited six months before receiving a reply. He politely said thank you, but they can't use my idea right now. A few months later, I read that they came out with a new series of dragon books and continued down the well-established path of dungeons and dragons. They found a niche that worked for them and they continued to pursue it.

My favorite editor quote is, "That's been done a dozen times No one wants to read a book about Elvis." Or, "No one's ever written a book about your subject. Give us something proven."

Write from your heart and produce the best book you are capable of. The world needs to hear your story.

17.
Therapy- Because You Can't Help Yourself

That's why I write. Call it OCBD (Obsessive Compulsive Book Disorder) or a simple obsession, but when I get an idea flowing, I can't stop until I'm finished.

But when I am finished, I feel a great sense of peace and relief because I birthed a new idea, and was able to formulate my idea into a collection of organized words stamped between the covers of a book.

That book idea in your head will drive you crazy unless you get it in print.

18.
More Options Than Ever Before

CreateSpace, Lulu, iUniverse, Innovo, Lightning Source and Book Surge are just a few of the great companies offering help with your publishing plan. Go to cnet.com for an excellent review of CreateSpace by David Carnoy Feb 5, 2009.
http://reviews.cnet.com/self-publishing/

He summarizes by saying, "Self-publishing is a fluid business. Self-publishing is a rapidly evolving industry with lots of competitors that are constantly throwing out new information. Publishers are continually upgrading their facilities, infrastructure, and pricing, and what I--or other pundits say today--could be wrong just a few months from now. Last year, Amazon was only offering 35 percent royalties on e-books. This summer, it goes up to 70 percent. What does next year hold in store?"

The only guarantee in business is that change will come. Some pundits predict that traditional publishing will be as extinct as a Brontosaurus in a few years, while other means of information sharing will grow exponentially.

Visualize an eBook reader as thin as a sheet of paper containing all the books in your local library. Public domain books will be free for all, but for a small subscription fee, you can download and read the latest bestsellers at your convenience.

19.
The World Has Changed.

When you and I weren't looking, a new generation of bloggers, twitterers, texters, facebookers, and downloaders sprouted up in all corners of the known world.

This week the federal government expanded the electronic airways to provide 500MHz of broadband space for our use. The electronic age is here and it's time to jump on the ever-growing stream of new information and grab a few megabytes of digital space.

The world is changing faster than ever before.

Hold on tight, and enjoy the ride!

20.

Fun, Excitement and Adventure

Remember the first scene in the *Twilight Zone* move back in 1983? Dan Aykroyd turns toward the driver in the front seat and says, "Do you want to see something really scary." The drive nods in anticipation, and Aykroyd changes into a weird monster and scares his friend half to death. The scene ends, and your mind is left to fill in the horrid details of what happened next.

Self-publishing is a similar experience. Daily you ride the roller coaster of anticipation, joy, failure, regret, excitement, satisfaction, hope and fear.

If nothing else, at least it will add excitement to your life.

Jumping into publishing is a new adventure that will lead to you into the uncharted realms of your mind.

> *Writers are not just people who sit down and write. They hazard themselves. Every time you compose a book your composition of yourself is at stake.*
> *~E.L. Doctorow*

10

More Help

CreateSpace Fee for Service –Book Service

Enclosed is a partial list of book services from CreateSpace which may help you layout and publish your book. I have never used any of the services CreateSpace offers, so I cannot give a review on their qualifications or value.

Supported Interior PDF

You've designed and prepared your own interior PDF file and now you're ready to begin the publishing process. We can assist you to ensure your file meets our submission requirements and help get your files finalized for publication.

Price: $149.00

Author's Advantage Book Interior

A well designed book interior can enhance the professional appearance of your book. With this service you'll choose from a variety of interior design options to help achieve a layout that reflects your book's personality and style.

Price: $249.00

Total Design Freedom Custom Book Interior

Looking to make your book truly unique? Graphic designers will incorporate your ideas and vision into your book's interior, giving it a customized look and feel through layout, typography, and formatting.

Price: $379.00

Total Design Freedom Children's Book Interior

With distinctive fonts, eye-catching colors, and unique touches that carry your themes throughout your book, a Total Design Freedom Children's Book Interior helps your story resonate with readers of all ages. Work with our design team to create an interior layout for your book that complements your artwork and captures young imaginations.

Price: $379.00

Kindle-Ready File Conversion

Have us create a digital version of your book to reach new customers. Our Kindle-Ready File Conversion service converts your paperback book into an eBook for Amazon.com's Kindle wireless reading device.

Price: $69.00*
* Books with complex formatting, e.g. mathematical formulas, tables, and heavy graphics, or trim sizes exceeding 7"x10" require additional fees. In rare cases, we may not be able to convert your book.

Custom Illustrations

Give your book a colorful edge with striking illustrations by a talented and experienced artist. The artist will create original artwork for your book based on your story and the mood you'd like to create.

Price: $225.00 per illustration (minimum of 5 illustrations)

Supported Cover PDF

You've designed and prepared your own cover PDF file and now you're ready to begin the publishing process. We can assist you to ensure your file meets our submission requirements and help get your files finalized for publication.

Price: $99.00

Author's Advantage Book Cover

Have your own image you'd like to use on your book's cover, but still want professional help with the layout and formatting? Let us create a market-worthy book cover based on your design selections, incorporating your image and author photo.

Price: $149.00

Unique Book Cover

Work with our professional design team to custom-create an affordable, striking cover that broadcasts your book's key messages with distinct colors, fonts, and one central image.

Price: $349.00

Signature Book Cover

Give your book every opportunity to shine with a Signature Book Cover! Our professional design team will custom-create an expressive, engaging book cover that helps convey your book's nuanced messages using a variety of images, colors, and textures.

Price: $749.00

Illustrated Book Cover

Work with a professional artist to create a unique illustration that helps bring your work to life.

Price: $949.00

Book Scanning

Have a previously published book that you want to bring back to market? Make your book available for sale using our scanning services.

Interior Scanning: $99.00
    Plus $0.50 per black & white text-only page and $10.00 per grayscale or color page Cover Scanning: $99.00

Great books to buy
Guerrilla Marketing for Writers: 100 No-Cost, Low-Cost Weapons for Selling Your Work by Jay Conrad Levinson, Rick Frishman, Michael Larsen, and David L. Hancock

Self-Publishing And Marketing From The Trenches - Paperback (Nov. 12, 2009) by Peter H. Zindler

Dan Poynter's Self-Publishing Manual, 16th Edition: How to Write, Print and Sell Your Own Book (Self Publishing Manual) by Dan Poynter

1001 Ways to Market Your Book by John Kremer

The Elements of Style: 50th Anniversary Edition by William Strunk and E. B. White

A Writer's Reference with 2009 MLA Update - Plastic Comb (July 6, 2009) by Diana Hacker

Little, Brown Handbook (11th Edition) by H. Ramsey Fowler and Jane E. Aaron.

Great Websites to visit

www.selfpublishingreview.com
The Self-Publishing Review is an online magazine devoted to self-publishing: book reviews, publisher reviews, interviews, news, opinion, and how to's.

The aim of this site is to legitimize self-publishing – not just as a fallback plan, but as an avenue that's increasingly necessary and useful in a competitive publishing industry.

If the site has a manifesto it is to improve the culture around self-publishing.

www.writersdigest.com

Each issue of Writer's Digest brings you the must-know tips and publishing secrets you'll need such as:

* Technique Articles geared toward specific genres
* Business Information specifically for writers
* Tips & Tricks for rekindling your creative spark
* Inspirational Stories of writers who are living the dream, and how they got there
* The Latest (and Greatest!) Markets for print, online and e-publishing
* Tools of the Trade, including the latest advice and info on software, books and Web resources

www.publishingbasics.com/current/
Publishing Basics Newsletter

A Monthly Newsletter for the Small Press and Independent Self-Publisher || Published by Self Publishing, Inc.

ISBN information

www.bowkerlink.com.

Bowker is the best place to order an ISBN number for your books. However, if you want to save money, Create Space will provide a free ISBN number.

Microsoft Word Help

office.microsoft.com/en-us/word/fx100649251033.aspx

Free online lessons and videos for
Word 2000
Word 2002
Word 2003
Word 2007

thewriterssecret.wordpress.com

Byron's blog on writing, living life and self-publishing.

www.paypal.com

This is a leading third party credit card payment processor. PayPal was acquired by eBay a few years ago. Unlike merchant accounts, they do not charge minimum monthly fees, applications fees, leases, equipment purchases, etc. Their transactions fees are reasonable. However, their primary role is to process online transactions.

Google Adwords

www.adwords.google.com
This is a leading pay-per-click search engine service. Google has some great programs to generate more traffic and revenues from your web site.

You write to communicate to the hearts and minds of others what's burning inside you. And we edit to let the fire show through the smoke.
~Arthur Polotnik

11

Conclusion

There are hundreds of outlets available to help you publish your book. Some cost thousands of dollars and some cost very little. It's up to you to determine your skill level and your level of commitment.

When you start to self-publish you place yourself in the esteemed ranks of Lord Byron, e.e. cummings, Henry David Thoreau, T.S. Eliot, Benjamin Franklin, Zane Grey, Nathaniel Hawthorne, Carl Sandburg, Ernest Hemingway, Stephen King, Rudyard Kipling, Louis L'Amour, D.H. Lawrence, Rod McKuen, John Muir, Thomas Paine, Edgar Allen Poe, Alexander Pope, Beatrix Potter, Ezra Pound, Marcel Proust, Irma Rombauer, George Bernard Shaw, Upton Sinclair, William Strunk, Alfred Lord Tennyson, Leo Tolstoi, Mark Twain, Walt Whitman, and Virginia Woolf. *From John Kremer's Self-Publishing Hall of Fame*

I'd expect that all of these authors were told by someone they were wasting their time and money on such foolish ventures. I'd expect that you've heard the same.

We write because we love the process and publish because we believe we have something good to offer our readers.

Happy writing.

> *Let your writing journey be blessed, your edits few, and your thoughts pure.*
> *~Byron Mettler*

INDEX:

OUT of DARKNESS
A JOURNEY
BYRON METTLER

BYRON METTLER
SPEED KILLS!

CHANDLER
BY
BYRON METTLER

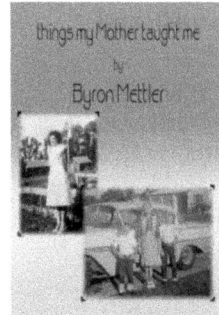

things my Mother taught me
by
Byron Mettler

More Books by Byron
Available at
www.booksbybyron.com

OAK CREEK ADVENTURE
BY
BYRON METTLER

sixteen
STORIES
by
John Howard Ladd

Compiled by Byron Mettler

50 GREAT BIBLE OBJECT LESSONS
By
Byron Mettler